Basic Principles
of Biblical Counselling

Basic Principles
of Biblical Counselling

Lawrence J. Crabb, Jr., Ph.D.

MarshallPickering
An Imprint of HarperCollinsPublishers

Marshall Pickering is an Imprint of
HarperCollins*Religious*
Part of HarperCollins*Publishers*
77–85 Fulham Palace Road, London W6 8JB

First published in the USA in 1975 by Zondervan
Publishing House and in Great Britain
in 1985 by Marshall Pickering
This edition published in Great Britain in
1997 by Marshall Pickering

1 3 5 7 9 10 8 6 4 2

A catalogue record for this book is
available from the British Library

ISBN 0551 03100X

Printed and bound in Great Britain by
Caledonian International Book Manufacturing Ltd, Glasgow

*To my parents
who have made 2 Timothy 3:14, 15
the key verses in my life*

Contents

Foreword

For several decades now, the writings of Dr Larry Crabb have been nourishing the Christian Church – especially when he has written on the theme of biblical counselling. I first came across Larry Crabb in 1980 when he invited me to be a guest at his week-long *Institute in Biblical Counselling*, which was run on that occasion in Boca Raton, Florida. Although I had previously been trained in counselling theory and practice, I came away from that week with insights that revolutionized my approach to counselling and have been the framework for my own thinking about people and their problems ever since.

Personally, I owe a great debt of gratitude to Larry Crabb, not only for convincing me of the sufficiency of Scripture in relation to counselling, but for the help and encouragement he has given me over the years in my attempts to develop effective biblical counselling here in the United Kingdom.

In addition to being a psychologist in private practice, Dr Crabb has served as Chairman of the Biblical Counselling Department at Grace Theological Seminary in Winona Lake, Indiana, USA, and later as Professor of Counselling at Colorado Christian University. Recently he has resigned from this position and although he still endorses all counsellor training programmes that have a strong biblical base, his present burden is to help ordinary Christians of all churches to be able to relate to one another in such a way that 'scratches where others may be itching'.

The thing I love about Dr Crabb's writings is the preponderating influence which Scripture has in his thinking. Here is a scientist with a keen and fertile mind yet willing to subject himself and his findings to the judgment bar of Scripture. Perhaps his biggest contribution to the kingdom of God has been the clear model he presents for applying in-depth counselling to the local church. For far too long we have failed to utilize the resources which God has placed in our local Christian communities – resources which if properly utilized could bring about a transformation in effective daily living. If every minister and Christian counsellor were to digest and apply the principles set out in this book, the Christian Church would, I believe, become a far better agency for caring than it is at present.

Rev Selwyn Hughes

Waverley Abbey House, Farnham, Surrey
October 1996

Preface

A FEW YEARS AGO I sensed the leading of the Lord to leave secular employment and to establish a distinctly Christian psychological ministry. With barely enough faith to move an anthill, I questioned whether God could meet the material needs of our family in some way other than through a weekly paycheck. Other concerns, hopefully more mature, about the specific will of God for my life, became in a fresh way the subject of intense, prayerful interest. During those months of thinking through the direction my professional life was to take, I was greatly helped and motivated by the close friendship and wise, persistent counsel of Rev. David Nicholas, pastor of Spanish River Presbyterian Church in Boca Raton, Florida. Sensing a faith in need of encouragement, Rev. Nicholas arranged for a year-long stipend to enable me to leave secular employment and to collect my ideas on what the Bible says about counseling. This book is the visible product of that year.

I wish to publicly express my sincere appreciation to Rev. Nicholas for his unselfish concern and interest in my ministry and for his continuing encouragement throughout the months of putting my thinking on paper. I also want to acknowledge my indebtedness and gratitude to the following people who, through their material support, provided me with the time to organize my thoughts into book form: Dr. and Mrs. Kenneth Fulton, Mr. and Mrs. William Hallman, Mr. Ford Mason, Mr. John Peachey, Mr. and Mrs. Chuck Perry, Mr. and Mrs. Lawrence Werch, Mr. and Mrs. Robert West, and Mr. and Mrs. Norman Wymbs.

My secretary, Bebby Weigand, receives my special thanks for patiently typing and retyping the manuscript until I exhausted my compulsion for revisions.

And to my wife Rachael (who wonderfully fills her role as helpmeet, which in our case often includes the difficult job of counseling a counselor), I express my deepest love for her support and patience during the months when I was preoccupied with writing.

Lawrence J. Crabb, Jr., Ph.D.
Boca Raton, Florida

Introduction

WHEN I RECEIVED MY Ph.D. in clinical psychology, I assumed that I knew how to counsel people with problems. Experience, I anticipated, would sharpen my technique and add detail to my understanding of psychological difficulties. As I involved myself in regular counseling (both in a university setting and in private practice), I slowly became aware of a deep sense of uneasiness hidden behind my confident professional manner. In moments of painful honesty, I had to admit that I had very little confidence in what I was doing. At first I quieted this inner disturbance by reminding myself that I was young, that experience would solve the problem. But the nagging sense that something was wrong, something requiring an upheaval in my thinking, continued to press for attention.

I closed my textbooks and sat back in my chair to ask — What exactly was I doing in my counseling office? Divorcing myself as best as I could from technical theory and jargon (which often seemed to camouflage confusion), I asked myself what was really wrong with the people who were asking me for help. What sort of help did they really need? Why was I somehow unable to swallow without choking the answers offered in my textbooks? Certainly the range of theoretical positions to choose from was broad enough (there were almost as many theories as there were textbooks). Surely I should be able to comfortably plug into one of the theories and assume a fixed professional orientation. As I restudied what I had learned in graduate school, it became clearly and frighteningly apparent that most of what I was believing and doing as a professional psychologist was built upon the swaying foundation of humanism, a fervent belief in the self-sufficiency of man. As a Christian committed to a biblical view of man, I could not make the psychological thinking in which I had been trained dovetail with basic biblical beliefs like the fall of man, his separation from God, his desperate need of divine assistance, the promise of love, joy, and peace to those who accepted the free gift of

13

eternal life through Jesus' substitutionary death and who learned to live in the power of the Holy Spirit. The truths of Christianity seemed to have little bearing on the activities in my counseling office and were at many points flatly contradicted by my professionally orthodox behavior. And that disturbed me.

I determined that my belief in Scripture was rational and firm (the writings of C. S. Lewis and Francis Schaeffer were most helpful in persuading me that Christianity is intellectually compelling) and that my psychological theory and practice would have to conform to biblical truth. In an effort to define a truly Christian approach to counseling, I began reading the works of evangelical Christian psychologists and psychiatrists. The more I read the more difficult it became to block out the impression that, with a few rewarding exceptions, humanistic psychology was not being *replaced* by Christianity but rather *integrated with* certain biblical ideas. Althouth the adequacy and supremacy of Jesus Christ often were asserted, the discussion of problems and solutions seemed to rely upon the wisdom and power of man. I earnestly desired a substantial understanding of the problems of people and of the best ways to deal with them which could rightfully claim to be thoroughly biblical.

Prayerful and intense thinking about my counseling efforts has resulted in the sketching of a preliminary model for counseling theory and practice which I believe to be consistent with biblical revelation. I have presented the model both in my counseling office to clients and in workshops on biblical counseling to interested Christians. The response has encouraged me to submit my ideas to a larger audience for scrutiny and reaction. Many questions remain unanswered. I regard my thinking as embryonic rather than final. It is my hope that this book will be used to bring us closer to a precise understanding of and dependence upon the complete sufficiency of our Lord Jesus Christ, especially in the counseling office.

Basic Principles
of Biblical Counseling

1

Broadening Our Vision

MOST PEOPLE HAVE problems. Some don't get along with their husbands or wives, some are worried sick about money or their kids, many are depressed or nervous, others just feel empty inside and unfulfilled, still others have problems with alcohol or sex. There are not enough professional counselors to handle all the problems. Even if there were, few people could afford the expensive and lengthy series of sessions often involved in traditional professional counseling. It must be admitted further that the success record of psychologists and psychiatrists does not justify the confidence that affordable professional therapy available to all is the answer.

The increase in personal problems and a growing disillusionment with professional efforts to solve them have resulted in an openness to other approaches. The timing is right for Christians who take God seriously to develop a biblical approach to counseling which asserts the authority of Scripture and the necessity and adequacy of Christ. Bitterness, guilt, worry, resentment, anger, self-pity, envy, and lust are eating away at the spiritual (and often the physical) lives of people. In the back of our minds, we Christians have privately thought that commitment to Christ and dependence upon the power and leading of the Holy Spirit should really be what the doctor orders. But secular psychology and psychiatry have sold us on the notion that emotional problems are the result of psychological malfunctioning and hence are the unique province of the psychological specialist. O. Hobart Mowrer, noted psychologist, has indicted the church for selling its spiritual birthright of teaching people how to live effectively to the sometimes antagonistic brother of psychiatry for a mess of propaganda pottage.

I am convinced that the local church should and can successfully assume responsibility within its ranks for restoring troubled people to full, productive, creative lives. One psychiatrist recently commented that his patients are all basically hungry for love and acceptance. Where should true love be more evident than in a Christ-centered local church? Jesus prayed that His people would be one. Paul speaks of rejoicing and weeping with one another and bearing each other's burdens. To the degree that the Lord's design for His Church is implemented, the deep need for love, which if unmet generates psychological problems, will be satisfied within the Church.

As will be discussed in more detail later, people need not only love but also a purpose for living. Life must have meaning, a purpose, and a goal that is neither self-produced nor temporary. Again the local church is designed to meet that need. The Holy Spirit has distributed spiritual gifts to each member of the body. The exercise of those gifts contributes to the most important activity going on in the world today, the building of the Church of Jesus Christ. What a magnificent, eternally significant purpose for living is available specifically within the framework of the local church. I will later discuss more thoroughly my belief that the local church was uniquely designed by God to minister to the needs of emotionally upset people.

If we are to hope for success in such an immense and seriously neglected responsibility, pastors need to return to the biblical model not of ministering to their people but of equipping their people to minister to each other by using their spiritual gifts. Congregations need to regain that wonderful sense of "koinonia" fellowship and to practice true community. Pastors need also to understand the scriptural perspective on personal problems and to reinforce biblical counseling efforts from the pulpit. Men and women in the Church should be trained for the unique ministry of biblical counseling. The development of the local church into a counseling community employing its unique resources of fellowship and ministry is an exciting concept which needs further thinking. As a basis for such thinking, the obvious question needs to be answered. What is a biblical approach to counseling? Urgent, intelligent, and widespread attention must be devoted to developing an approach to helping people that is consistent at every point with Scripture.

Every concept of biblical counseling must build upon the fundamental premise that there really is an infinite and personal God who has revealed Himself propositionally in the written word, the Bible, and personally in the living word, Jesus Christ. According to the testimony of both, the most basic problem of every human being is his separation from God, a gulf made necessary by the fact that God is holy and we are not. Until this chasm is bridged, people may temporarily and partially solve their personal problems by approximating biblical principles but they can never possess an absolutely satisfying life now nor eternal life hereafter. The only way to find God and to enjoy life with Him is through Jesus Christ. When we agree with God that we are sinful, repent of our sins, and trust in Jesus' blood as full payment of our sins' penalty, it brings us into an intimate relationship with God (a staggering fact) and opens the door to vital living.

Now if Christians are to realize the vision of displacing secular counseling with a biblical approach operating within the local church, we must neither minimize these doctrinal essentials nor stop with them. Evangelicals often do one or the other. It simply is not enough to inform a depressed person that he is sinful and that he must confess his sin to Christ and stop living sinfully. Such an approach presents Christianity as oppressive rather than liberating, an insensitive system of hard-to-keep rules. Recent efforts to outline a Christian approach to counseling seem to envision the counseling process as something like a witch hunt: locate the sin and burn it. I will discuss later why I believe that this approach, although accurate in its fundamentals, is inadequate and not truly biblical. It is a serious error to suppose that Christ is helpful only in distinctly spiritual matters but is irrelevant in resolving personal problems (like depression), and to then look to secular psychotherapy for answers. Those who simply and repeatedly assert that "Jesus is the answer" usually are not grappling hand to hand and soul to soul with troubled lives. When they are confronted with the reality of personal, emotional, or family distress, they either encourage more trusting, praying, and Bible study (good advice but often no more useful than telling a sick person to get medicine) or they shift gears and go to the other extreme: "Your problems are not spiritual; they are mental. I cannot help you. Better get some professional help."

We must develop a solidly biblical approach to counseling, one which draws from secular psychology without betraying its Scriptural premise, one which realistically faces the deep (and not so deep) problems of people and honestly evaluates its success in dealing with them, and, most importantly, one which clings passionately and unswervingly to belief in an inerrant Bible and an all-sufficient Christ.

The first part of the book is addressed to those who regularly advise troubled Christians to "seek professional help." Although secular professional counseling can be helpful, it often operates according to basic theoretical positions which diametrically oppose Scripture. A number of positions representative of the thinking of secular psychology are reviewed and critiqued from a biblical perspective.

The rest of the book introduces my conception of a truly biblical approach to counseling.

2

Confusion in Counseling

BEFORE PEOPLE WILL listen to a solution, they must know there is a problem. In this chapter and the next, I want to bring the problem into focus by discussing the current situation in secular psychology. Man's best efforts to build a tower into heaven always fall short. Engineering skill, theoretical genius, and hard work have gone into the tower of psychology with impressive results. But until we see that they fall short of their goal we will not be much interested in an alternative approach.

We live in a day when distinctions are blurred: opposites are blended into a hybrid that is neither one nor the other, and ecumenical compromise is hailed as proof of love and open-mindedness. Distinctions between male and female are disappearing into unisex — pretty men and rugged women. Concepts of right and wrong (formerly thought to be opposites) have now been blended into a relative morality where right may sometimes be wrong and wrong may sometimes be right. Assertions of religious truth have been broadened to accommodate antagonistic points of view within a single, elastic framework. Underlying these phenomena is the widely assumed belief that there are no absolutes, no fixed reality external to a person which, because it is true, simply refuses to bend under all pressure. Abandoning belief in absolutes has inevitably resulted in mass confusion. Everyone has an idea as to how things should be and there is no external, absolute standard against which the validity of any idea can be measured. Nowhere is the proliferation of differing untestable notions more appallingly evident than in psychologists' offices.

In 1959 a book was published entitled *Psychoanalysis and Psychotherapy, 36 Systems*. If an updated sequel were to be written today, at least double that number of counseling approaches could be identified. When you go on to consider that each systematic approach is modified by the personality, style, background, and bias of the counselor, you are faced with the disturbing thought (perhaps exaggerated but only mildly) that there are as many approaches to counseling as there are counselors. And yet we continue to speak as though the word "counseling" refers to an identifiable and reasonably uniform entity or process. I know of one couple who went for "counseling," were badly burned by their experience, and have therefore refused to ever see a "counselor" again. What they do not realize is that another counselor may think and talk so differently from the first as to defy comparison.

The obvious need in the field of counseling is a clearly stated unity within which there is room for diversity. In other words, we must have a fixed framework, an established set of unchanging and meaningful truths which will tie together the varied elements which fall within its boundaries. Francis Schaeffer speaks of form and freedom in the local church. The Bible specifies a fixed form, a rigid set of limits. Within the prescribed form, there is room for considerable freedom depending on the circumstances of the moment, the participants, and a host of other factors. In the absence of form, freedom is unchecked and unguided, and flourishes into randomness and utter confusion.

24

(Confusion, it should be noted, sometimes is cured by dogmatism.)

Psychologists often dignify confusion with the label "eclectic." But without the solid foundation of a true, unchanging understanding of man and his problems, eclecticism can become a technical disguise for sloppiness and guesswork. There is simply no hope for achieving meaningful diversity (or, as one psychologist calls it, "technical eclecticism") until a unity has been established. True freedom can exist only within certain and meaningful form.

Until recently it was thought that the necessary unity could be developed through scientific research. But many admit now that the scientific research method is inherently inadequate for the job of defining truth. Science can provide neither proof nor meaning. In another paper,[1] I pointed out that modern philosophers of science confess the incurable impotency of science to ever say anything conclusively. Science can assess probability but can take us no further. To reach certainty demands that we go beyond (not deny) reason and exercise faith. Humanistic optimism that man is sufficient to solve his problems has crumbled under the weight of science's inability to clearly assert that any single proposition is true. We need proven universals. Science cannot provide them. We must in faith reach beyond ourselves to get what we need.

Faith ultimately has two options from which to choose. When philosophical questions are understood properly, the range of possible answers becomes small. The well-stated ultimate question that Sartre posed, "Why is it that there is something rather than nothing?" can be answered finally in one of only two possible ways: either there is a personal God, one who thinks, feels, and chooses, or there is an impersonal god, more of a thing than a he, something which in the absence of personality operates randomly according to the principle of chance. Stated somewhat differently, either our world was designed by an infinite Designer or it accidentally happened by pure chance. These are the two options which faith may embrace. There is no other. The unity so necessary for bringing order out of the chaos of counseling approaches must depend either on God or on chance. If chance is the ultimate reality, observed order is accidental, prediction becomes impossible, and systematic efforts to counsel according to previously observed patterns becomes logically (though perhaps not practically) indefensible. To counsel in a manner consistent with disbelief in God means to counsel in a manner consistent with belief in chance and nothing more. Were a counselor to do that, his practice would come to a sudden end. No therapist, nor any other person for that matter, really behaves as if chance were the ultimate reality. Now that leaves them in the uncomfortable position of living as though God were there but refusing to take direction from Him. One of the Huxleys once said that although there is no God, things work a lot better if we believe in one. Counseling works better if counselors assume order, predictability, and responsibility, phenomena which probabilistically should not exist unless there is a personal God.

All counselors do of course assume the existence of a certain ordered structure (e.g. Piaget's built-in structures of mental functioning) and can operate effectively to the degree that their assumed framework of universals corresponds to what really is there. Scientific methodology is able to increase our confidence that we have hold of some portion of reality by experimentally detecting what seem to be invariant elements in human nature. No one seriously disputes that some form of order exists and is capable of observation and description. The important question is whether the order is logically meaningful.

Denying the existence of God and thereby (at least implicitly) accepting an ultimately random universe has two necessary results which often are overlooked: *one*, we would probabilis-

26

tically expect to observe far less order in the world than we do (order from chaos is less likely than chaos from chaos); *two*, whatever order we do find must be seen as a random (although truly ordered) occurrence. The only meaning which a random event (no matter how orderly) can justly claim is a present, existential meaning: "This is what is right now. It is a real present experience." The most you can say about what exists right now is that it exists right now.[2] Order in a chance universe carries no implications about how things *should* be; it merely describes how things are and how things respond to certain forces. The best way to proceed with the observed order is in no way determined by the order itself. And yet every counselor desires to do something with the order he sees. If a counselor is to move in a meaningful direction with a client, he must have a persuasive reason for moving one way and not another. If he is to defend his planned movement as "right" or "good," he must appeal to something outside the order with which he is working. But if, when he looks outside his set of observed regularities, he finds nothing but chance (or, as Schaeffer puts it, he finds no one home in the universe), he has no logical basis whatever for recommending a specific course of action. There is no logically meaningful reason for doing anything. Order in a chance universe merely is. It leads nowhere. It is finally meaningless. Psychology apart from God can never provide a meaningful framework for movement in the counseling office.

In a sentence, my argument is this: the field of counseling needs a certain and meaningful unity. Science by itself can provide neither. It can attach greater or lesser probability to hypotheses but it can never prove a single proposition. It can describe an observed regularity in human nature but it falls short of establishing any structure as truly meaningful. In every case, a counselor selects and chooses his procedures according to a theory, often an implicit and poorly defined theory, but a theory nonetheless. If that theory is not tied down to the ultimate reality of God, diversity in technique does not move freely within a certain and meaningful form.

The thought behind this book is quite simple: if there really is a personal God, then there is a truth about people and their problems which can provide the necessary foundation or framework for variety in counseling technique. And basic truth apart from God cannot be known with certainty apart from revelation. And so it becomes the task of the Christian psychologist to provide a universally true and meaningful understanding of people that derives from biblical revelation. When revelation is discounted as a source of truth, we are closed up to uncertainty. The next chapter discusses what has happened in psychology because God's revelation has been ignored.

[1]"Data and Dogma as Compatible," in *Christianity Today*, Volume XV, No. 12, March 12, 1971.

[2]The emphasis on experiencing the present moment characteristic of the modern encounter group movement looks like an updated version of the old philosophy, "Eat, drink, and be merry, for tomorrow we die." The only meaning available is in the radical now.

3

Floating Anchors

CHRISTIANS SOMETIMES ARE quick to support anyone who degrades the wisdom of man and asserts the sufficiency of Scripture as a base for all thinking. Dismissing all secular thinking as profitless denies the obvious fact that all true knowledge comes from God. It is clear that God has given men minds and that He blesses mental exercise with increased understanding of His creation.

Psychologists have been exercising their minds for years and have come up with a great deal of useful information and techniques, such as intelligence tests and ways to help a stutterer stop stuttering. They have contributed enormously to our understanding of such things as why people respond as they do to certain forms of stimuli, of how people think and how thinking relates to action and emotions, and of the developmental stages which children pass through. I do not want anyone to interpret this chapter as a cavalier dismissal of secular psychology. I believe psychology as a thoroughly secular discipline (like dentistry or engineering) has real value. My concern is to identify the basic assumptions about people and their problems implicitly advocated by secular psychology, and in the light of Scripture to see these assumptions as totally inadequate as a reliable, fixed framework for counseling. Only Scripture can provide the needed structure. Psychology's efforts, while enlightening in many ways, are about as useful to the counselor in search of an absolute foundation as floating anchors are to a ship in stormy waters.

Diagram 1 oversimplifies but accurately summarizes the essential thinking of five representative theories of mental health. Each position explains the basic problem of people and suggests a solution. In the diagram, each circle symbolizes man. This chapter discusses each theory in enough detail to support the judgment that none of them provides a foundation for counseling compatible with biblical revelation.

SIGMUND FREUD

Freud is interesting to study for several reasons. Prior to his day, personal or emotional problems were generally attributed either to demon possession or to undetected organic defect. Responsibility for cure fell either to the exorcist or physician. Freud pried the lid off the mind and opened a Pandora's box of fear, envy, resentment, lust, aggression, and hatred. Years of intensive study convinced Freud that at the center of the human personality were two basic drives pressing for gratification, the drive toward sensual pleasure (eros) and the drive toward power and destruction (thanatos). When these drives were denied expression, Freud asserted, emotional problems developed. Stated in another way, Freud was saying that the primary motivation of people is self-gratification. People are basically out for themselves. The minus sign in the circle (see Diagram 1) represents selfishness. But, Freud added (and the slash marks in the circle indicate), most people don't know they are selfish or, more precisely, they do not acknowledge the self-serving motivation behind their actions. They dress up their selfish motives in noble clothing: "I just want

DIAGRAM 1:

PROBLEM	SOLUTION	RESULT
Freud		
Unconscious Selfishness; Harsh Conscience *(handwritten: Selfish)*	Soften Conscience Uncover Id	1. At best: Socially acceptable hedonism 2. At worst: sociopathy
Ego Psychology		
Weak Ego Dominant Id	Strong Ego Controlled Id	1. At best: pride 2. At worst: frustration
Rogers		
Inhibited Goodness	Liberated Goodness	1. At best: temporarily workable relativism 2. At worst: unrestrained hedonism and lawlessness
Skinner *(handwritten: Environmental input / organism output)*		
Random Control	Systematic Control	1. At best: mechanical adjustment 2. At worst: technocratic tyranny; the end of man as man
Existentialism		
Rational Gloom and hopelessness	Non-rational hope	1. At best: self-sustained meaning 2. At worst: despair

what's best for him" says the wife who refuses to accept her husband as he is and pushes him to change. The real motivation goes underground into the unconscious in order to protect the superego (conscience) from being offended.

Now let me say all this a bit more technically. The neurotic webs which people weave represent distorted efforts to satisfy their own desires in a way that does not violate standards internalized by the conscience. Anxiety, for Freud the underlying factor in all psychological disorder, occurs when an unacceptable impulse ("I would like to kill my father because I hate him so much") becomes so strong that the individual is almost forced to consciously admit its existence. Danger signals warning of an impending clash between one's selfish desires (collectively labeled the id) and one's value system (conscience or superego) are subjectively felt as anxiety.

To this point there is a rough parallel with the biblical view. According to Scripture, man does live for himself; he insists upon directing his own life in a way that he believes will bring him happiness. "Every man did that which was right (i.e what he believed would meet his needs) in his own eyes" (Judg. 21:25). People are motivated to fill their empty insides but in ways which they determine rather than by following God's counsel. Correspondence between the Freudian view and the biblical view is suddenly disrupted when the solution to the problem is considered. In order to cure the problem of hidden selfish motivation, Freud proposes a three-step cure: (1) uncover the underlying motivation; (2) soften the conscience to the point where the motive of self-gratification is acceptable; (3) promote self-gratification within the bounds of reality and social acceptability. When a patient comes to see that all of his behavior is stained by selfishness at its motivational core, he may become upset. His emotional reaction to the insight that he is basically selfish is produced by an intolerant, rigid conscience. Weakening the conscience, lowering its standards to the point where selfishness is seen as biologically inevitable (man is merely a driven animal) and therefore at least tolerable, helps the patient resolve the tension between what he is and what he ought to be.

Mowrer has cogently pointed out that accepting the "is" and dismissing the "ought" leads to self-directed behavior without the check of moral restraint, a condition which psychologists call sociopathy. It can be seen that Freudian therapy essentially promotes living for oneself without the burden of a conscience. Step three covers this conscience-less behavior with the veneer of social acceptability. After doing away with a neurotically moralistic conscience, the patient accepts himself as a self-gratifying animal and proceeds to intelligently and purposefully go about the business of selfish drive-gratification in ways that do not create conflict with his world. Freud calls this living according to the reality principle as opposed to the pleasure principle. As a means of satisfying sexual urges, rape is inadvisable because it incurs society's wrath. Therefore find a cooperative partner or pay for it. Questions of morality are irrelevant. In the familiar id-ego-superego paradigm, behavior now takes into account the id (inner drives) and ego (contact with the world) and disregards the superego (contact with moral standards). At best, Freud encourages socially acceptable hedonism. Ultimately, Freudian therapy moves its patients toward sociopathy. Christians must completely reject the basic Freudian solution as amoral and anti-biblical.

EGO PSYCHOLOGY

Ego psychologists operate within the scope of Freudian theory but believe that Freud (especially in his earlier days) focused too much on the selfish, base part of man and failed to give sufficient attention to man's capacity for intelligent, adaptive self-guidance. Problems are viewed as the result of strong drives for self-gratification unchecked by a realistic, flexible ego. The

33

difference between the ego psychologist and the older classical Freudian position is one of emphasis. Ego psychologists are concerned with developing the potential for sensible, reasonable, decision-making behavior (ego structure) which can harness the brute drives and guide them into acceptable, productive channels. The circle in Diagram 1 includes a small plus sign, representing the weak but potentially strong ego. The job facing the ego psychologist is strengthening that adaptive capacity within man (building the ego) in order to equip him to chart a satisfying, fulfilling course for his life.

At this point, some Christians might be inclined to strongly assert that apart from God's enabling man does not have the means (no matter how well developed his ego may be) to live as he should. And that is of course true, but it is not a relevant objection to the ego psychologist's position. He is not saying that people by an act of their will can live according to the standards of conscience. He is rather stating that someone with a good self-image and realistic self-confidence can choose to arrange his life in such a way that his desires for pleasure and power will find reasonable satisfaction without conflicting seriously with his social environment. It can be seen that the ego psychological position is guilty of Freud's catastrophic error of stripping the moral conscience of any guidance function. The emphasis of ego psychology on adaptive functioning however invites a further biblical response (one which could have been offered to Freud but seems more clearly called for here). In their talk of adaptively meeting biological needs within a realistic social framework, the ego psychologists implicitly assume that man is *merely* a biological being with no primary needs other than biological. (It might be mentioned in passing that it is a logical absurdity to speak of true rationality [the sine qua non of ego functioning] in a randomly developed biological being. How mental operations escape assignment to the category of chance biological phenomena [which they must if one is to meaningfully label them rational] is difficult to conceive in a world without a personal Designer.)

The Biblicist will respond quickly that man is more than a biological being, that in fact he also is a personal being made in the image of a personal God. As a personal being, he has personal needs (a concept discussed later) which desperately require fulfillment if he is to enjoy or merely experience his status as a person. Because he is fallen and therefore separate from the personal God who alone can completely fulfill his personal needs, the man apart from God *must* remain less than fully human (that is, both biological and personal).

It can be seen then that the ego psychologist focuses the spotlight on biological needs and encourages adaptive self-reliance in meeting them. To the degree that his therapeutic procedures are successful, a proud sense of independence is promoted and the patient is further from God than before therapy. Inevitably however, because real personal needs remain unsatisfied, there will be a deep sense of emptiness and frustration. The familiar complaint, "Something's wrong; I can't put my finger on it, but I just don't feel like a whole person," will either surface or be suppressed by aggressive efforts at further self-reliance. The two possible outcomes of ego psychological counseling — pride or frustration — are hardly worthy objectives for a Biblical counselor.

CARL ROGERS

Next in the survey comes Carl Rogers, the dean of the encounter group movement in America. According to Rogers, Freud is wrong: man is not negative; the ego psychologists are wrong: man is not negative with a positive embryo awaiting development. Rogers likes to believe and firmly teaches that in the circle of man, there is only positive. All that is within is good. Corruption enters from without. People have an inherent self-actualizing tendency which when freed from restriction or forced channeling will lead to personal satisfaction and social harmony. This utopian dream (which must provoke an incredulous chuckle from any honest parent) is represented in Diagram 1 by a thick circle suggesting the rigid, moralistic, oppressive environment which blocks the inner goodness (plus sign) from expression. It occurs to me that Rogers might cure rebellion by eliminating rules to rebel against (without the law there is no knowledge of sin). When I follow that procedure with my children, the results are not in the direction of greater personal integration and family oneness. Perhaps Rogers would reply that I must keep on letting them express themselves, that whatever destructive misbehavior occurs is a response to subtly maintained environmental pressure, and that when inhibitions to total freedom are completely removed, I will then observe my child's true nature. I agree. It is that prospect which maintains me in my rule-enforcing behavior.

For Rogers all problems have their root in a failure to be oneself. The solution naturally is liberation. Relax the boundaries, implicitly trust the person, encourage self-expression of all that is within ("if you feel it, do it") and eventually the drive toward appropriate self-actualization will evidence itself in external and internal feelings of togetherness. Anxiety, viewed by most psychologists as the core of mental problems, results when internal visceral experiences (gut feelings) are denied assimilation into one's perceptual field (awareness) because of a learned negative evaluation. For example, I have been taught that hatred is bad (learned negative evaluation). When someone is mean to me (perhaps a rejecting parent), I automatically feel hatred (internal visceral experience). But because I value hatred as bad, I refuse to acknowledge that I am currently hating and so I "come apart" as a person. I separate the me I can accept from the me I really am. The strain of maintaining the separation is felt as anxiety.

The proper Christian response to Rogers is not to sneeringly reject all that he says as the ravings of a delusional optimist. Rogers has put his finger on a real problem among people, including many Christian people. Because Christians are supposed to love, we often do not admit it when we don't love — we fake it. Any hypocrisy separates a person from the reality of himself and reduces the new man in Christ to a fragmented phony. Rogers is profoundly correct in insisting that we acknowledge all that we are, including our gut feelings. He is tragically wrong in believing integration is best achieved by encouraging the expression of all that we are. To give in to my sinful feelings of hate is to separate me from my conscience and to grieve the indwelling Holy Spirit. Integration is wonderfully available to the person who honestly admits the hate, labels it as a fruit of the flesh, confesses it as sin, and learns to love in the power of God's Spirit.

Rogers is badly mistaken when he assumes that if left to myself with no direction I will always choose the best course of action. In so doing, he flatly denies the biblical teaching of a sinful nature. Scripture tells us that there is none good, no not one; that the wicked are estranged from the womb. Removing all externally imposed direction is an invitation to chaotic, self-willed behavior. Dorothy Sayres has said, "If you want your own way, God will let you have it. Hell is the enjoyment of one's own way forever." For a time it appears pleasant. Relativism is temporarily workable. It inevitably leads to absolute hedonism and lawlessness. Rogers believes that the results of letting people go their own way include joy, harmony, and love. Scripture claims that these qualities are the fruit of the Spirit, and describes the fruit of the flesh (going one's own way) in radically different terms. For a Christian counselor to adopt a Rogerian framework for his work is an open rebellion against Scripture. I want to say again however that rejecting everything Rogers says and does because his basic presuppositions are horribly wrong is by no means required of a Christian. As mentioned above, Rogers has clarified certain personality problems for which Scripture offers solutions. He also has contributed a great deal on the value of warmth, genuineness, and positive regard as necessary qualifications for an effective counselor. Scripture not only recognizes the importance of these attributes, it also provides a realistic basis for them.

B. F. SKINNER

B. F. Skinner is fourth on the list. In his view, man is not negative (Freud), he is not negative and positive (ego psychology), nor is he positive (Rogers). According to Skinner, man is really nothing, a big, empty zero. In his recent book, *Beyond Freedom and Dignity*, Skinner explicitly states and fervently insists that man is a totally controlled being. We would do well, he asserts, to bid good riddance to man qua man. His interpretation of laboratory data compels us to reject the fiction that man is a choosing, personal, initiating, responsible being. Such disproven myths are standing in the way of developing his mechanistic utopia. Man is no more than a complicated dog, absolutely determined by his environment down to every detail of his thinking, feeling, and doing. It should be noticed that the concept of determinism is not unique to Skinner. Freud taught that man is determined by internal dynamic forces beyond his control. Skinner dismisses Freudian dynamics as reified mental fictions and shifts the locus of control to physical, external forces (including genetic structure and physiological (chemical states). Christians need to react strongly to such teaching. Skinner is doing nothing less than robbing people of all significance. The entire concept of personal responsibility is absolutely emptied of meaning. The problem of crime is solved by defining it out of existence. We no longer have criminal people, we only have criminal environments. While Freud seeks to rearrange internal personality structure, Skinner wants to modify a person's environment in a way that will automatically change his behavior in a direction chosen by the modifier.

In Diagram 1, the arrows pointing into the circle represent environmental input. The arrows pointing away represent organism output, responses that follow predictably and inevitably from the input. The problem with people is that we are controlled in maladaptive ways by unnoticed and unplanned contingencies (people do whatever is followed by a reinforcing consequence). The cure is to identify the reinforcers that are controlling behavior and to systematically manipulate them to produce desired behavior. Reflect on this thinking for a few minutes. Notice that it reduces man to an impersonal collection of potential responses. I recently heard a Christian psychiatrist tell how he overcame "morning inertia," a sense of depression which made getting out of bed and going to work a difficult, burdensome labor every day. He ordered his morning to include hot coffee and a favorite pastry as soon as he reached his office as a reward for going to work. I have no objection to beginning one's day pleasantly. I am concerned when a Christian psychiatrist (who ought to know better) treats himself like a manipulable object rather than a child of God who should responsibly yield his day to the Lord and depend upon the indwelling Spirit for the power to respond to divine direction. To settle for a donut as motivation when the purpose and power of God are available is culpably foolish. As long as God's will is the foundation for a day, donuts and coffee may of course be a legitimate (and even somewhat motivating) morning pleasure.

Skinner's thinking at best results in the mechanical adjustment of a person who was never meant to respond mechanically. Eventually, the path Skinner would have us travel leads directly to a technocratic tyranny. An ultimate controller (or group of controllers) would assume control of all the primary reinforcers (food, clothing, shelter) and distribute them to people who behaved according to the master plan.

In a pamphlet entitled *Back to Freedom and Dignity*, Francis

Schaeffer points up two central difficulties in Skinner's thinking. First, if all people are really controlled, who will control the controller? Skinner's discussion of reciprocal control (we all control each other) evades the problem. If there is to be planned control of society, someone must be above control in order to selectively and purposefully control according to plan. But in Skinner's system, there are no free agents. No one qualifies for the job of controller. Everyone is controlled. Second, granted that control is possible, one must determine in what direction people should be changed. Any decision about change implicitly assumes a value system. But within Skinner's absolutely mechanistic, evolutionary system, there is no logical foundation for stating "this is right" or "that is wrong." As Schaeffer points out, the value system of the atheist necessarily reduces to Marquis de Sade's belief that whatever is, is right. Skinner dismisses this objection as needless polemic, and insists that we begin by asserting the self-evident value of survival. It is difficult to see how survival in a totally mechanistic, chance universe can be viewed as anything other than an incidental occurrence. Any positive feelings we have toward this accident of fate (or negative feelings for that matter) are themselves the product of blind chance and hence meaningless. Although it is not my purpose to explore it further, a few minutes thought will suggest the complexity of ethical problems which you would have even when the foundational value of survival is granted.

Christians must reject Skinner's teaching that man is no more than a complicated dog. Christ died for people because they are made in His image and have been granted real value as persons. The freedom of man to choose his direction is a concept clearly taught in Scripture and is a necessary one to vindicate God's righteousness in punishing sin. At a more practical level (I do not wish to comment on the sovereignty-free will issue; whichever theological position one adopts need not have significant bearing on the point I want to make), as a Christian counselor I hold my patients responsible for how they *choose* to live their lives. If they choose to ignore God's directions, they are blameworthy. I recognize their dignity and freedom. Responsibility for one's actions must not be shifted from the person to his environment. The husband who says "My wife refused me sex so I committed adultery" has partly explained his behavior, but he has not excused it. Responsibility for sin must be placed squarely on the sinner. It must never be shifted to one's circumstances, no matter how difficult they may be.

Christians are indebted to Skinner however for specifying the manner in which behavior is *influenced* (not controlled) by circumstances. In another paper I developed this thought at some length.[1] Let me again state that knowledge must not be rejected as non-Christian just because it springs from a non-Christian source. Skinner's work on conditioning includes true knowledge about how I relate to my world (as an active rather than passive agent) and can be used to advantage by a Christian counselor operating exclusively within a Christian framework. I do not agree with Jay Adams' wholesale dismissal of Skinnerian technology. In his *Handbook of Christian Counseling*, he talks of breaking habits by avoiding tempting circumstances. If you are a glutton, do not tempt yourself by walking by a bakery. Skinner has helpfully analyzed such temptation in his work on stimulus control. A Christian counselor familiar with Skinner's research would be in a better position to advise his client how to behave than one who had not familiarized himself with Skinner.

EXISTENTIALISM

The last theoretical position in Diagram 1 is less a unified view and more a loosely associated collection of ideas grouped under the broad heading of existentialism. The existentialist in my thinking comes closest of the five theorists to squarely facing up to the necessary implication of naturalism: if the cause is impersonal and therefore random, the result also must be impersonal and therefore random. Matter or energy, whatever impersonal beginning one chooses, can never rise above itself to produce something designed. There can be no design without a designer. And without design, there is nothing meaningful for reason to discover. Man becomes unknowable because there is nothing to be rationally known. In this view, man is a question mark. He obviously is something because he is there, but since he is a purely chance phenomena, there is nothing which reason can meaningfully say about him. He is an accident, an unplanned happening who obeys no laws and is headed in no intended direction. The existential psychologist says no more about man than "he is." But therapists like Victor Frankl are emphatically (and correctly) insistent that people can not live without purpose or direction. The basic problem with people according to Frankl is what he terms the noogenic neurosis, a crisis in meaning. People do not know who they are or why they are here. The existentialist does not seem to notice that it is at least curious that all people have randomly (by their theory) developed a need for meaning in a world which has none. This is either a strange and consistent cruel twist of fate (although the term "cruel" is emptied of evaluative significance in a random universe: what we call "cruel" merely is) or it is evidence for an objective meaning which is at least dimly apparent to every creature.

A careful study of Frankl's logotherapy makes it clear that Frankl does *not* subscribe to the theory of objective meaning. He rather solves the neurosis of meaninglessness by persuading its victims to arbitrarily lay hold of something for which to live. Since there is nothing objective or real which gives life meaning, his solution is reduced to blind faith: do something, feel something, be something, live for something and hope that this will provide you with the meaning you need. Perhaps the excitement of sex, the euphoria of drugs, the enchantment of music, the experience of freedom from any obligations, the rewards of education, of book writing, or of building hospitals, will provide the meaning so passionately desired. Whatever purpose you select for your life will have no rational foundation, since for the existentialist everything is absurd. The proposed solution clearly becomes a non-rational attempt to live happily. Nonrational hope will embrace anything which by an act of the will can provide temporary meaning. But people are persistently rational. We think. We ask questions. We look for answers. Thinking abruptly knocks the props from under whatever purpose in life we have erected. And because we all eventually think (even the most simplistic person is aware of a desire to rationally know), the existentialist solution inevitably crumbles into utter despair: there is no meaning and I must forever remain a question mark, an unhappy misfit produced by sadistic accident to need something which I can never have.

Christians must loudly assert that our faith is based on facts, not feelings. The whole Christian system rests upon the historicity of Jesus Christ, His literal identity as God, His real death and bodily resurrection. Christianity begins with a personal God who provides objective meaning. Man is not a question mark. He is in fact made in the image of God. He is a fallen being. Whether he feels these things or believes them to be true does not affect their reality status. They are objective truths which can be discussed and known rationally. Man's problem is that he has chosen as a free moral agent in a designed universe to wilfully assert his own right to supremacy and self-determination. He therefore is really separated by sin from the one source of true meaning. In the Christian view man's noogenic neurosis is a real thing which allows only one solution in our meaningful but fallen world. The solution to man's dilemma is not hope in the "Gee, I hope this works" sense. Biblical hope is never a nonrational attempt to ignore the conclusions of thinking. It is rather a certain, communicable, propositional set of truths which is rooted in the birth, life, death, and resurrection of Jesus Christ and which deals rationally and logically with the objective problem of sin. Christian counselors are always dealing with a known quantity. There is never any doubt about the direction a person must move if he is to truly resolve his problem. Christians are not free to recommend that a client find his own solution. They must always direct their clients toward conformity with biblical truth.

Freud said that man is selfish and one ought to first know it, then accept it as OK. Ego psychology claims that man can be strengthened to successfully rechannel selfishness into personally and socially acceptable outlets. Rogers denies any inner badness and teaches that man is filled with goodness and should therefore let it all hang out. Skinner contends that man is neither good nor bad, that he is a complicated mass of responses which in terms of intrinsic value amounts to a large zero. Since man can be controlled, let experts (Skinnerian psychologists) control him toward ends desired ultimately by the controller who himself is totally controlled (a random vicious circle with no breaking in point). Existentialists don't know if man is bad (Freud), good (Rogers), both (ego psychologists), or neither (Skinner). Man is logically absurd but needs something besides rational meaninglessness; therefore leave rationality behind and blindly hope that some experience will fill the void.

Scientific methodology is not adequate to establish the validity of any one view of man's basic nature. Without the weight of certainty, each system is a floating anchor. Selecting a basic position on the nature of man, the universal so badly needed in the field of counseling, resembles a random throw at the dart board unless some objective source of knowledge is available. To find certainty, there is simply no avenue to pursue but revelation.

[1]*The Scientist and Ethical Decision;* Charles Hatfield, ed., Inter-Varsity Press, 1973.

4

An Aerial View

PSYCHOLOGISTS HAVE A reliable knack for complicating the simple. But Christians sometimes are guilty of oversimplifying matters that really are quite complex. A useful discussion of the nature of people, why their lives are often in shambles, how the problems develop, and the Christ-centered path out of ineffective living to abundant life must necessarily involve some complexity, less than Freudians think but perhaps more than "read, pray and trust" type Christians suppose. In an effort to make the required complexity more understandable, I want to sketch the general approach which the rest of this book develops in more detail.

People with problems usually complain about their feelings. "I feel depressed"; "My wife really makes me mad"; "I feel so hurt when my husband ignores me"; "I worry all the time; I'm just so upset." Counselors often encourage the expression of more feelings and entertain the optimistic hope that if enough negative feelings are gushingly poured out, the person then will be rid of his emotional problem. I heard one counselor encourage a troubled client to freely express her hate toward her parents, to "get the poison out of your system." Other counselors look for the cause of the feelings in some external circumstance responsible for producing and locking in a negative emotion. A counselor may tell his client, "You are angry because your wife refused to go along with your decision," or "Your hostile feelings toward women are the result of a rejecting, cold mother."

Neither approach seems to me to be consistent with Scripture. Paul taught that transformation comes from renewing neither feelings nor circumstances, but our minds. Encouraging catharsis as a curative end in itself fails to acknowledge the reality of a sinful nature which has a limitless supply of negative feelings. Looking for the cause of an internal emotional problem in an external circumstance strips the individual of responsibility for his problems and flatly contradicts the Lord's teaching that it is not what enters into a man that defiles him but what proceeds *from* within.

When one is experiencing the fruit of the Holy Spirit, he certainly does not feel bitter, contentious, angry, or jealous. Paul teaches that these feelings are properly regarded as the fruit of the flesh. The biblical counselor will respond to the problem feelings by identifying the situations in which these feelings are strongest and then looking carefully at the client's behavior in these situations. He is expecting to find behavior patterns that reflect the operation of the flesh. For example, if a husband complains of anger toward his wife, the counselor would ask him to be specific about when he feels most angry. It may be that his wife frequently throws together a skimpy, unimaginative supper at the last minute. Without excusing the wife's behavior, attention would then be directed away from both the wife's behavior and the husband's emotional response and focused on the husband's actual behavior when he sits down to his tasteless meal. Perhaps he expresses his irritation openly: "Why don't you try being a wife for a change? Thanks for nothing." Or maybe he is the quiet, smoldering type who coolly ignores his wife for the rest of the evening. In most cases it will not be difficult to pinpoint specific behavior well designed to promote friction and reduce harmony.

Many Christians who counsel believe that at this point both the feeling and the behavior should be forcefully identified as sinful. The client must recognize that he is violating the biblical principle of "love your wife as Christ loved the church" (in other words, no matter how badly she treats you, love her: "God commendeth his love toward us in that while we were yet sinners — utterly unlovable — Christ died for us"). Counseling, in this view, then becomes an exhortation to confess, repent, and change. Transformation is assumed to depend upon a renewing of behavior.

There is a difficulty with such a limited view of counseling. Certainly clients can confess, repent, and responsibly change. Before the Lord they are obliged to do so. The difficulty with this approach arises when one realizes that a person's sinful feeling and sinful behavior reveal something quite specific about his sin nature which if unchallenged could cause further trouble at a later date. In chapter 7 I will develop the idea that the content of the sin nature is in the mind. Another way of saying it is that sin begins in the thought world. Underneath feeling and behavior is belief. If the feelings and behaviors are sinful, the belief behind them must be wrong.

The husband in our previous example may implicitly hold the wrong belief that "I can be fulfilled in my marriage only if my wife exhibits devotion to me and thus makes me feel important." He then would be granting his wife the power to make him happy or unhappy. Because he also probably believes (as most of us do) that he has a right to happiness, he will regard his wife's neglectful behavior as a violation of his rights. Angry feelings and words naturally flow from such thinking. Although the husband may be persuaded to confess his anger as sin and to make efforts to change his behavior, if his beliefs remain uncorrected, the probability is dangerously high that he will become angry again next week and

49

the next and the next. I believe that a failure to identify and correct wrong thinking is responsible for much of the repeated failure of people who sincerely try to live the Christian life.

In every instance, the wrong thinking will involve the sinful belief that something more than God (and what he chooses to provide) is necessary for meeting one's needs. A renewed mind is one which renews the belief that was held at the point of salvation: God is totally sufficient for me. But we often say, "I need to have my way in order to be happy." As long as a person believes that, he will not be able to thankfully accept his circumstances when they go counter to his way. He will rather resent them (get mad at his wife), kick against them (tell her off), and engage in depression-producing self-pity ("I sure got stuck with her"). After the biblical counselor identifies and challenges the wrong thinking responsible for the unloving behavior and the troublesome feeling, he must then encourage new behavior consistent with right thinking. He may tell the husband, "Look, God says that He is sufficient for you. Your need to feel important depends not on your wife's devotion but on your exercising your spiritual gift. Are you doing that?" New behaviors including some form of ministry in the church, more responsible action on the job, and loving behavior toward his wife, would then produce the fruit of the Holy Spirit, the wonderful experience of love and joy and peace.

The entire process can be summarized in a simple diagram sketching the six steps of counseling.

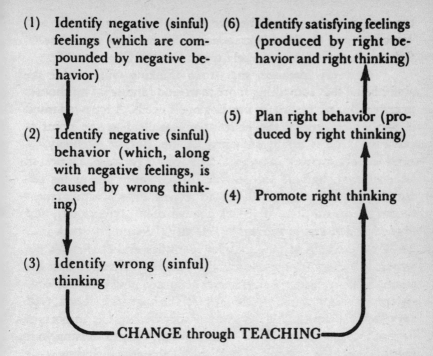

(1) Identify negative (sinful) feelings (which are compounded by negative behavior)

(2) Identify negative (sinful) behavior (which, along with negative feelings, is caused by wrong thinking)

(3) Identify wrong (sinful) thinking

(4) Promote right thinking

(5) Plan right behavior (produced by right thinking)

(6) Identify satisfying feelings (produced by right behavior and right thinking)

CHANGE through TEACHING

In this model, the crucial step involves changing the client's thinking, renewing his mind. If it is true that our thought processes (what will we fill our minds with) largely determine how we behave and what we feel, we must devote considerable attention to this whole matter of wrong thinking. Thinking always has content. We always think about something. In order to understand wrong thinking, we must therefore first consider the subject matter about which people think incorrectly. And that is the subject of the next two chapters.

5

Understanding Our
Deepest Needs: I

AFTER READING THE review of secular psychological thinking, the
Christian reader hopefully is now convinced (if he wasn't before)
that confusion can give way to order only by an appeal to revelation as the foundation for a counseling strategy. God's written
revelation makes it insistently clear that any right thinking about
the problems of people must begin by recognizing that man is not
now in a normal condition. He is fallen from the norm. He has
missed the mark. He is a sinner. Paul begins his inspired treatise
to the Romans on basic Christian theology by forcefully asserting
the truth that man has separated himself from God by willful
rebellion. He concludes his introduction by insisting that every
one must absolutely shut up when facing God. We are guilty. We
have no defense. After acknowledging our guilty, helpless condition, we find our mouths stopped as we tremble in God's presence,
waiting to see what He will do, fearful that He will do what
righteousness demands and eternally turn His face from us. An
appreciation of the reality of sin is a critically necessary beginning
point for an understanding of the Christian view of anything. A
psychology worthy of the adjective "Christian" must not set the

problem of sin in parallel line with other problems or redefine it into a neurosis or psychological kink.

The effect of sin is separation. Four distinct separations summarize the total catastrophe introduced by man's willful rebellion. First, man is separated from God — he has spiritual problems. Second, he is separated from his fellows — he has social/interpersonal problems. Third, he is separated from nature — he has ecological and physical problems. Fourth, he is separated from himself — he has psychological problems. Christians understand that the *ultimate* cause of every difficulty is sin, a decision to live life without regard for God's authority.

In recent years, some Christians have gathered strength from the writings of psychological notables like O. Hobart Mowrer and Thomas Szasz and have boldly asserted that there is no such thing as mental disease. Mental problems are better thought of as dis-ease, the realistic discomfort of guilt occasioned by sin. These folks teach that troubled people are uncomfortable with themselves because of real, moral guilt over definite personal sin; they are living ineffective, anxiety-ridden lives because of sinful patterns of behavior. Biblical counseling is being heralded (and I want to be one of the trumpeters) as a long-awaited approach which certainly should and perhaps eventually will replace the false religion of professional psychotherapy which claims to bring love, joy, peace, patience, and self-control into the lives of distraught persons without any thought whatsoever of the Holy Spirit of God.

I am concerned that in the appropriately enthusiastic reception granted to the concept of biblical counseling a certain gentle sensitivity to deep human needs may be lost. Assertions that people are sinful, not sick, may promote a harsh confrontational approach which misses the person and the unmet needs aching within. It is true that counselors often need to cut through the layers of emotional complaints to expose the core problem of a sinful pattern of living which underlies the presenting problem. As soon as these patterns are clearly identified, it is tempting for the counselor to proceed immediately with a program of authoritative rebuke ("that behavior pattern is sinful") and exhortation ("you must repent, confess, and change"). With the thought obsessively ringing in his ears, "There is no such thing as mental illness, only sinful living," the counselor sometimes models his counseling efforts (as was mentioned earlier) along the lines of a witchhunt with an eventual burning.

Without retreating an inch on the position that people are responsible for their own problems by living sinfully, I believe that the biblical counselor needs to look a little deeper into the thinking behind the choice to live sinfully. Jay Adams' simplistic assumption that specific personal guilt over definite willful sin is behind all emotional distress misses the more basic problem. Behavior always moves toward a goal. People choose to do wrong things on the basis of faulty thinking about how to reach a goal. Unless that wrong thinking is corrected, the faulty thinker will continue to make similar wrong choices which he wrongly believes will meet his needs. There is more to real counseling than rebuke and exhortation. Teaching a new way of thinking, correcting wrong ways of thinking which underlie wrong behavior and wrong feelings is central. Short term success and eventual relapse (or joyless, labored maintenance under continued exhortation) is the predictable result of merely exhortational counseling.

In the following discussion, I will develop the notion that every person must first reach the goal of personal fulfillment. Until that goal is reached, man is not free to live for something or someone else. People have deep personal needs which must be met. In this chapter and the next I will sketch what I take to be the biblical view of man and his personal needs. In chapter 7 I will discuss the process of thinking and put forward the view that all personal problems are really thinking or belief problems, wrong beliefs about how to meet those needs.

A Christian view of the needs of people must always begin with the understanding that man is made in the image of God. To clearly identify what that means requires the recognition that the God of the Bible is infinite and personal. An infinite God is a noncontingent being, that is, He depends on nothing outside of Himself for His existence. The ultimate problem of metaphysics (why is there something rather than nothing) demands an appeal to an infinite beginning. The critical question whose answer will shape every aspect of our thinking about people and their problems is whether this infinite beginning is personal or impersonal. If it is impersonal, then everything (including this sentence) is a purely chance phenomena and can claim neither importance nor meaning. If a personal God is denied (as Francis Schaeffer points out), whatever exists must then be seen as the product of the impersonal plus time plus chance and nothing more. The moment someone insists that his thinking is true to what really is or the moment a person claims to need love or a purpose in life, he has added to the formula. Some sort of design, a hint of personality, something more than absolute chance is introduced. Skinner denies that the beginning is personal and so he is shut up to the principle of randomness. And yet he does two curious things. First, he conducts experiments to discern the regularities in our universe and then repeats his experiment to make sure he has identified a stable regularity. A world operating with no higher law than chance would most likely not be an ordered world subject to repeated measurement. Second, he asserts that his theories are somehow true and should be implemented in practical ways in our society. In a world with an impersonal beginning, there is no knowable truth. Every assertion is a random occurrence based on random cerebral motions; Skinner's assertions are no exception. To proselyte for one's own program presumes that there is a right way or a better way to do things. But again, without an external truth and an intended pattern as to how things should be, we are left only to personal preference ("I happen to prefer hitting people to being nice") with no adequate reason for stating that one person's preference is somehow better than another's. The reply that things work better if a certain pattern is followed presumes a value decision about what "better" means. And an adequate answer can be given only when there is an infinite reference point which is personal. Without laboring the point further, let me insist that belief in an infinite and personal God is at least a practical (and to my mind intellectual) r.ecessity. Once you grant that there is a God who is both infinite and personal, you can move to a clear understanding of the needs of people.

If God is both infinite and personal, and if man is somehow made in His image (which I will assume rather than take the time to defend), then man becomes a noninfinite (the infinite cannot create the infinite; the fact of creation defines the created being as contingent on his creator) and yet personal being. Since man cannot be infinite like God, then "made in His image" must mean that man is personal just as God is personal. Man then is a physical, contingent, finite being on the one hand and a genuinely personal being on the other. As a finite creature, he has needs, for example, food. Without food man physically dies. He desperately and absolutely requires food if he is to continue his existence as a physically living creature. (It is interesting to note that freedom in this context is best defined as the ability to be true to what really is, to adaptively fit into reality. There is no such thing as absolute freedom. I am free to jump off a tall building. But I am a slave to gravity. Freedom in any meaningful sense means the free choice not to jump off a tall building and so to avoid the ill effects of gravity.)

But man is more than physical. He is also personal. And as a personal being, he has personal needs. Unless these needs are met, he will die as a person. I have heard the heartbreaking lament many times in my office "I just don't even feel like a person." Physical needs often are well met and yet there is an emptiness, a deep sense of discontent which often is palliated by satisfying physical needs to the point of gluttony.

In order to understand biblical counseling, we must identify clearly the deepest personal needs of people. Here is where the heart of the trouble really lies. Most psychological symptoms (anxiety, depression, uncontrolled temper, pathological lying, sexual problems, irrational fears, manic highs) are either the direct result of or defensive attempts to cope with unmet personal needs. (However, there are cases where the symptoms are organic.) Scripture gives us insight into our personal needs in the instruction on child training: "Fathers, provoke not your children to anger, lest they be discouraged" (Col. 3:21). "Discouraged" carries the idea of "broken in spirit," completely disillusioned about oneself, having no inward sense of personal worth whatsoever. Proverbs asks, "A wounded spirit who can bear?" (Prov. 18:14). Although there is a kind of brokenness which God in His mercy inflicts in order to bring man to a realization of his hopeless condition apart from God, Paul is suggesting in Colossians that when *man* breaks the spirit of another, the results are disastrous. When God breaks me, He has all the resources necessary to put me back together as a new creature in Him. When I am broken by another or when I fail to turn to God for rebuilding, I remain a shattered, fragmented, fatally wounded personality. *The basic personal need of each personal being is to regard himself as a worthwhile human being.* Nothing is sinful about the need to be worthwhile. God (as we shall see in a moment) has made wonderfully available the necessary and sufficient provision for meeting that need. To love oneself in the sense of regarding God as unnecessary and the self as sufficient is sin and results in personal death. To accept oneself as a worthwhile creature is absolutely necessary for effective, spiritual, joyful living.

Some who have patiently waded through the book thus far may be asking when I will get to the "practical stuff": how do you help a depressed person? what do you say? how often should you talk with them? etc. It must be remembered that a physician studies anatomy before he sets a broken leg. Basic personality functions all depend upon meeting the central need to regard oneself as worthwhile. Effective counseling demands a clear understanding of this need.

I should parenthetically mention that I have carefully avoided the phrase "people need to *feel* worthwhile." I may examine the evidence and conclude that I am worthwhile in Christ without *feeling* especially good about myself. The feelings come as I step out on faith, believing the evidence and acting on the strength of my beliefs. Notice that the order is the same one we established in chapter 4: correct the beliefs, align the behavior with the beliefs, then enjoy the resultant good feelings: fact-faith-feeling. Any variation from that order will not work.

If a sense of personal worth is critical to effective living, if all personal problems which confront biblical counselors are the result of a failure to meet that need, we must understand precisely how a person can come to regard himself or herself as worthwhile.

SIGNIFICANCE

In order to experience the deep conviction that "I am worthwhile," each of us must be rationally aware of two elements in his or her life. The first of these is significance, a purpose for living which will give me a real and lasting impact on my world and a purpose which I am completely adequate to accomplish. Secular psychologists have consistently identified this need as basic. Viktor Frankl speaks of the noetic part of the personality which longs for a reason for one's existence. He spent a number of years in a concentration camp and was struck by the fact that the men who made it through without psychologically crumbling were men who were living for some definite purpose (perhaps a family, an occupational goal, finishing a book, etc.).

Bruno Bettlheim, who has worked extensively with autistic children, describes a simple three-stage process of psychological development. First, a child learns to name things: "chair," "table," "mommy." Second, he becomes aware of a relationship between these parts of his world: "When the chair is pushed against the table, it stops." Third, he looks for ways to become part of his world, to be the cause in a cause-effect sequence. Intentionality develops. He notices that mother consistently pays loud attention to him when he spills the milk. When he wants attention, he then learns to spill the milk with subtle deliberateness. He is now having an impact on his world. He matters. He causes an effect. He has the beginnings of significance. He can see that he makes a visible difference in his world. Children who never develop to the third stage suffer psychological problems. Why? They do not enjoy significance and hence have no basis for regarding themselves as worthwhile.

In *Power and Innocence*, Rollo May suggests that the frustrated need for causal impact leads to aggression and violence. University students who have been depersonalized by a culture which respects things more than people, systems more than students, lash out in acts of violence. Their behavior is inexcusable and deserves the strictest disciplinary control. Yet it will not do to simply call them rebels and sinners (although the labels are accurate) and let it go at that. Beneath the sinful confusion of the student rioting of the 1960s were deep, unfulfilled needs for personal importance and significance, for a purpose worth dying for, for meaning that can stand rational scrutiny, for clear, constructive, lasting impact. Burning a building or disrupting academic functioning with a sit-in does give one a sense of immediate impact and offers the attraction of working for a goal. Christians must hold people responsible for lawless behavior, but we must do more. We must go underneath the behavior and identify their deep personal needs. Then we must provide them with real answers to their legitimate questions: "What should I live for? How can I find true personal significance?"

Meeting Significance Needs

Rogerian-style humanists teach that we are important because we are humans. Skinnerians subject the statement "I need to be worthwhile" to a functional analysis to determine what environmental input will yield the verbal output, "I am significant." They attach no substantive reality at all to the internal need (remember, in their system man is only physical, not personal) and so solve the problem of finding personal worth by denying its existence. Freudians tend to treat the problem of worth as symptomatic of frustrated physical drives for pleasure or power. In a reductionistic system where nothing is real but matter, personal needs are reducible to physical needs. Existentialists like Frankl seem to recognize the validity of need for meaning (even though their godless presuppositions make any such need a meaningless accident with no rational hope for fulfillment) and encourage each person to work out his own solutions.

Every provision of secular man for meeting the real need for personal significance is logically and horribly inadequate. Let me explain why. (If you are not philosophically oriented, read this part slowly but please do *not* skip it. Biblical counselors must be able to intelligently assert and defend the proposition that Christ really is the necessary and sufficient answer for the needs of people. Otherwise they may come across as blindly dogmatic and unconvincing. Christianity, when rationally presented, is neither blind nor unconvincing.) In chapter 1, I suggested what Schaeffer has discussed rather thoroughly in *He Is There and He Is Not Silent*, that final reality *must* be either a personal God or an impersonal god.

If I assume that God is impersonal, I must go on to say that without a personal beginning there can be no design. And without design there can be no purpose or goal, no planned movement toward an intended end point. The position that there is no personal God requires one to assert that pure random chance is the ultimate governing reality.

Jean Paul Sartre has observed that a finite point requires an infinite reference point if it is to have meaning. Said in another way, a finite point derives its meaning from its context. Now (and here is the critical thought) if the finite point of my life or any single unit within that point exists in the context of an impersonal god (or at least not in the conscious context of a personal God), its meaning becomes identical to its context. My life becomes a random occurrence, an accident headed nowhere, a chance phenomena without real meaning or significance. But I cannot live with that. I do have real personal needs which must be met or I die as a person. And so I choose not to think so deeply and to set short-term goals (home, car, family, income, position, whatever). I immerse myself in these externals. As long as I keep frantically busy (or drunk, or asleep) and avoid asking real questions, I experience a facsimile of significance which temporarily (though incompletely) meets my needs. Christians sometimes are puzzled by the many non-Christians who seem to function reasonably well when some believers literally crack up. In order to enjoy psychological health, people must meet their need for significance. Non-believers (and many Christians too) do gain non-lasting significance from short-term goals and so function reasonably well. In their moments of honest self-examination, most admit to a sense of "something's wrong down deep." Lacking explanations or answers, they ignore their deep, quiet uneasiness and redouble their efforts to gain significance from reaching temporal goals.

Paul was not ashamed of Christianity because he realized

it was dynamite. It transformed dead people into live people, weak people into powerful people, and empty people longing for significance into deeply fulfilled people satisfied with the real purpose and importance available through Christ. Paul hints at the Christian resources for meeting significance needs in Romans. In the first chapter and twenty-first verse, he tells us the first wrong turn that people make which leads to utter degeneracy and personal death: they fail to glorify God as God.

God is glorified when I bow humbly before Him, acknowledging His right to run my life, and bringing myself into line with my Creator as His obedient creature. Accepting Christ's death as payment for my sins puts me in a position where I can center my life in the context of His will. I am alive to Him, indwelt by the Holy Spirit, who works in me "both to do and to will of his good pleasure" (Phil. 2:13). Now each moment of life, each unit of behavior (getting out of bed, playing ball with my kids, kissing my wife) can be seen as part of a larger meaningful whole. The context of my life becomes the eternal purpose of the sovereign God of the universe. Because a finite point derives its meaning from its context, my life as a whole and in every detail can intelligently claim to be truly significant as a part of the exciting purpose of God Himself. Biblical counselors must grasp this point and see it as fundamentally important.

When someone says, "I'm a nobody; I really don't matter," a Christian must not respond with humanistic hot air like, "Oh, but you do matter. You are a human being and that makes you significant." Without a biblical foundation, that sentence is logically absurd. Neither must a Christian counselor offer a simplistic, biblical-sounding answer like, "Look, stop feeling sorry for yourself. Get on with living for others and serving God and repent of this sinful preoccupation with yourself and your self-concept." Understanding the fact that man made in God's image is a personal being and really needs to be significant, a biblical counselor will respond by saying, "It must feel terrible to think yourself so unimportant. You are right for being concerned with this problem. And I have great news for you. God designed you with the need to feel important and has provided an exciting way to deeply and fully meet that need. Do you want God's solution to your real problem? Let's take a look at what God's plan is for you in your present circumstances. If you will follow His plan and do what He wants you to do, you will experience the exhilarating sense of being a real somebody, a carefully designed and eternally meaningful child of God."

In Ephesians 4 Paul speaks of the body of Christ, the true Church, as growing according to the effective operation of each member. Other portions of Scripture (e.g. Rom. 12, 1 Cor. 12) teach that every born-again believer is gifted by the Holy Spirit to contribute to the growth of the Church. God has a definite purpose for each individual, a foreordained program for accomplishing His sovereign purpose through every member of His body (Eph. 2:10). In Christ, God has provided every person with significance, a meaningful purpose for living.

One of the hallmarks of the "church renewal" movement of our day is an emphasis on the gifted ministry. The pastor is not the only one gifted to work in the local church. Ordination is not required as a prerequisite for the ministry, or, perhaps a better way of saying it, God has ordained every Christian to the ministry. In a real sense, there are no Christian laymen. Every Christian is a priest and minister before God with the responsibility and privilege first to worship God directly and then to serve Him according to the gift He has given. I believe that God has designed the local church as the primary vehicle through which people are to exercise their significance-providing gifts. Pastors need to return to the model of Ephesians 4:11, 12, and equip their people for the ministry so that the plumber, schoolteacher, housewife, and professional can enjoy the significance of helping to build the eternal Church of Jesus Christ. As long as pastors do all the work in the local church, they are robbing their people of an opportunity to meet their needs as God intended.

Two further aspects of the biblical answer to significance should be mentioned. In whatever role God calls me to, He will equip me to function adequately. I must see myself as adequate in Christ. When I come home at night and my wife greets me with a worried look as she tells me about a problem with one of the kids, I feel a sudden sense of inadequacy. I am the head of the house, Paul tells me, and I am responsible to decide what to do. But I do not feel adequate for the job. So I pray, "Lord, give me wisdom. Amen." I still *feel* inadequate. I am not aware of a sudden surge of wisdom as a result of my prayer. At this point I must disregard my feelings and go again to my beliefs. God promises wisdom to perform the responsibilities He calls me to. I believe it. And so I act on faith. I think, listen to my wife, think again, then decide — even as I tremble with feelings of inadequacy. I must decide on the strength of my belief that God will accomplish His will through me, even if I make a bad decision. As I continue to practice faith by acting on my beliefs, the gratifying feelings of adequacy come. Again, notice the order: fact, faith, feeling or, in the terms I have used before, belief, behavior, feeling. If Christian husbands would grasp the thoughts in this paragraph, they would not renege on their biblical responsibility to involve themselves intimately with their families as the loving authority.

A second aspect of adequacy and significance has to do with self-acceptance. Many people go through life believing "I could accept myself as a worthwhile person if I were smarter, better looking, more athletic, more talented, etc." When a Christian grasps the truth that God has designed him perfectly to fit His purpose, and when he sets his will to be in the center of God's will, self-acceptance becomes a natural outgrowth of thanksgiving to God for His perfect planning. The matter of self-acceptance is important enough to merit more attention than the scope of this book allows. Perhaps further volumes will deal more thoroughly with the Christian's route to real self-acceptance.

In brief summary, let me state that people must accept themselves as adequate in a truly significant role if they are to honestly regard themselves as worthwhile and so to enjoy the fulfillment of being a real person. The need to be significant can be met only by glorifying God in my life by surrendering to Him. As I live in the center of His will, He provides the adequacy to perform the work. I accept myself as perfectly designed for the work, and I experience fulfillment as I engage in the eternally significant purpose of building the Church of Jesus Christ. I want to emphasize again that the exercise of spiritual gift in the local church is the most natural strategy for involving myself in deeply meaningful activity and to thus meet my need for significance.

6

Understanding Our
Deepest Needs: II

In ORDER TO regard themselves as worthwhile, people need not
only significance but also the security of being loved. Christianity
is essentially the drama of a relationship. It is a love story which
begins with a divorce. Our earliest parents spurned the love of
their Creator-Companion. But that left them empty. Not only did
they cut themselves off from a life of purpose and significance, they
also cut themselves off from the love which their inmost being
desperately required. Because God is love, He did not stop loving.
He immediately illustrated His plan to provide a path back to
Himself so that the relationship of love could be reestablished
forever. Paul shouts with joy the thrilling fact that nothing can
separate us from the love of God.

I recently spoke with a Christian woman who was sure
God had stopped loving her. She felt desperately insecure. Her
behavior over the past few years would certainly have turned me
off but fortunately she had Someone more faithful and loving than
I to depend on. I asked her to read Romans 8:32, 33. She wept as it
slowly dawned on her that she could not make God stop loving
her, even if she were to dedicate herself to that task for the rest of

her life. (It is interesting and somewhat unnerving to contemplate the richness of Paul's command to husbands to love their wives as Christ loved the Church.) Even while I was yet a sinner, spiritually dead and hostile to God, He loved me, sought me out, and constrained me by His inexplicable love to come to Himself. People need that kind of love. We need, really need, to be loved as we are, loved at our worst. We need to regard ourselves as worthwhile. In order to do so, we must not only be significant but also be secure in the unconditional love of another person. We need relationship.

Most people are familiar with the true story that took place in a nursery orphanage. Physically healthy babies were mysteriously dying. No one could account for the deaths of these children who were physically well cared for. Someone eventually observed that there seemed to be a direct correlation between personal loving attention and physical health. The children who lived were the cuter ones who were picked up more often by the orphanage personnel. "Professional mothers" were hired to cuddle the babies, holding them close and warmly, gently caressing them. The babies lived. The mystery was solved. Human beings desperately need to be loved.

People generally operate in one of two ways to meet their security needs. Sometimes, we put our worst foot forward to test the sincerity of those who say they love us. A teen-age girl who was terribly afraid that she was unloveable had the disconcerting habit of becoming very mean to anyone who showed a warm interest in her. When they withdrew from her, she was confirmed in her fear that she would never be loved. Counseling provided her with someone who continued to care regardless of her behavior. Although I never excused her behavior and refused to accept irresponsibility, through God's enabling I continued to love her with Christ's love and repeatedly reminded her that she would never quench the Lord's love.

A more typical (and more rational) approach to meeting security needs is putting our best foot forward in order to gain acceptance. This approach seems to work better than the first but the cost is high. After a time of intentionally trying to win approval, we become trapped in the necessity of continually parading our acceptable points and carefully concealing our unacceptable weaknesses. Recently a woman who had left her husband revealed in our first session an incredible history of sexual deviance, including adultery, incest, and lesbianism. I learned that after our session she literally trembled with insecurity. Facts which for so long had been carefully concealed, she spilled in a sudden emotional gush. She feared that such a list of unacceptable behavior would certainly cause me to utterly reject her. So often we try to be good *in order to be* accepted. Christians need to lay hold of the liberating truth that we are now free to be good *because* we are already accepted just as we are by an infinite Person who through His death has credited us with total acceptability.

I once spoke with a Christian woman who had been married for many years to a critical, harsh, unloving man. She had dried up personally, starved for the security of being loved. In her deep, personal agony, she had turned to another married man for love. So strong was her need to be loved and so gratifying was the experience of a warm, caring relationship that she had successfully rationalized her behavior as God's will. After all, doesn't God want us to be happy? How should a biblical counselor respond? To gently say, "Yes, you need love. If you feel more secure with another man, go to him" would absolutely contradict biblical teaching and be totally unacceptable. To sternly rebuke, "You are engaged in a sinful pattern of living. You must repent and confess. Return to your husband and learn to submit" would not help her at all with her real need to be loved. Equipped with an understanding of her personal nature and her deep personal need for love, a biblical counselor would quietly, firmly, and lovingly state, "You are right to be concerned with your need for love. God built you with that deep need and intends that it be met. Our job will be to understand how God plans to meet your need for security *within* the limits of His revealed will concerning marriage and morality. If you are willing to believe that God does love you and wants your best, you will trust Him enough to repent of your sinful behavior and return to your husband. Let's take a look at what God wants you to be as a wife and try to understand how He will meet your needs through your obedience to Him."

MEETING SECURITY NEEDS

We need a clear understanding of precisely how God wants to meet our need for security. Christians have no difficulty in talking about the sufficiency of Christ. To radically depend on Him to meet every need is quite another matter. Without noticing what is happening, sincere believers drift away from absolute reliance on the Lord, and while continuing to assert the adequacy of Jesus, begin looking to others *rather than* to the Lord for satisfaction of their personal needs. The radical premise of my argument is that we literally need nothing but the Lord and what He chooses to provide. In a brief article analyzing depression a Christian psychologist denied that premise by implicitly assuming that dependency on another person for meeting security needs is valid. He pointed out that depressives are typically dependent people whose security needs are not being met by the ones on whom they are depending for acceptance and love. When needs are not met, there is hurt. When there is hurt, anger toward the source of hurt (a desire to hurt the hurter) is predictable and usual. But the dependent person will not express his anger because he fears losing what little acceptance there may be. The anger though is still there and·because it has to be aimed somewhere, it is redirected toward the self. The result is depression. I have no quarrel with this basic formulation. My concern is with the suggested cure. He suggests that since the problem is anger directed inward, the cure would be anger directed outward. Teach the depressed person how to express his anger acceptably. Paul's command to "Be angry and sin not" is offered as biblical sanction for the advice. Now it certainly is true that anger expressed in biblically guided efforts to correct a wrong situation can be healthy and constructive. But it seems to me that a central problem of critical importance is not directly dealt with by this counseling strategy. The problem is not the anger; the real culprit (from a biblical view) is misplaced dependency. The person who is angry at another for not loving him is assuming that he *needs* that person's love in order to regard himself as worthwhile.

It is of course legitimate to want another's love and to want it so much that its absence will occasion real grief and suffering. But I must never slip into assuming that I *need* that person's love in order to meet my basic need for security. If that assumption is true, then God is not at that moment meeting the needs of His child. Has God proven unfaithful? The depressed person's assumption is mistaken. It is not in touch with the reality of God and His love. I literally need nothing other than what God allows me to have. But, some will reply, God had nothing to do with the other person's free choice to sinfully reject me. Although it is certainly true that God is never the author of sin, that objection introduces a frightening situation. Now I cannot trust God to so order my circumstances that He can work all things together for my good. Sinful man can thwart God's loving purpose to provide for my every need. I must hope that the people in my world choose to cooperate with God's plans or my need for love will remain unmet. What a horrible and unthinkable state of affairs.

When the omnipotence and sovereignty of God are even feebly apprehended, I relax. God will meet my needs. No one can stop His love or the plans of His love. I am in His hands and there

I rest secure. When someone whom I love rejects me, I may respond with deep concern and grief over the severance of a personal relationship. But if I respond with a personal hurt caused by a threat to my basic security, if hurt leads to anger, if I am inwardly saying, "You haven't met my needs and that makes me mad," then I am believing that in order to have my personal need for security met, I must have this person's love, something which for the moment God has not provided. And that is a false belief. Either God has failed me or He hasn't. Either He is meeting my needs right now or He isn't. Christianity demands that I trust God to be faithful. If I really did need that person's love, God would see to it that I had it. If I do not have it, I do not need it, although its absence might cause profound feelings of loss. (Unless you believe with your whole being that there really is a God, this argument is hopelessly circular.) When I depend upon God's provision for my needs, and not on what I *may think I need*, I will respond to rejection not with anger but with deliberate thanksgiving in the midst of my sorrow. And it will be sincere. So many at this point will say, "Be thankful for so and so's rejection? Maybe I could bring myself to say 'thank you' but I surely wouldn't mean it." But if my mind is fixed on the staggering truth that the sovereign God of the universe loves me and has pledged Himself to provide me with everything I need, if I really believe that, then I will sincerely (sometimes with *great* difficulty but still sincerely) bow my knees in thanksgiving when I experience the rejection of another, not because God's love compensates for that rejection but because God's love can work through that rejection.

Christians often have a gooey, romanticized view of God's love which is really saying, "I will believe you love me if I can have my way, if I can do what I want to do, be what I want to be, and have what I want to have." God is seen as less of a father and more of a spineless, kind, indulgent heavenly grandfather. When something goes wrong, we feel that God has stopped loving us or surely

72

He wouldn't have allowed this to happen. The truth of the matter is that God never has loved us with that kind of love in the first place. His love relentlessly pursues our best, even when we would happily settle for less. God is in the business of sanctifying and purifying me. Although I am absolutely forgiven and enjoy a Father-son relationship with Him which will never change, I am still a sin-stained problem. God loves me enough to straighten me out, to smooth off the rough edges, to chip away until the brilliance of His Son shines through my life. Sometimes the sanctifying process is painful. When in the midst of trouble I long for God to love me, I often am asking for reprieve from difficult circumstances. If I understand God's love, I will know that I am really asking that God love me less. "Let me alone. I don't want to be refined anymore through tribulation. Turn down the heat on Your burning love which is shaping me through searing pain into the image of Jesus Christ. Agree with me to settle for second best. Love me less." And this He cannot and will not do. He will always desire my best and He will one day present me holy and without blemish. The cleaning up process is sometimes difficult. It might include rejection by another. When that happens, I am to believe by faith that God is loving me through that event and respond with thanksgiving, not specifically for the rejection but for the continuing operation of God's love which can make that rejection work for my good.

Job was a likely candidate for depression. Although he went through horrible trials and suffered the deepest anguish of soul, the record suggests that he never suffered from the kind of depression which is brought on by anger toward his world redirected inward. And yet his world had fallen apart. Material wealth, physical health, family were all stripped away. To express anger over the losses rather than bottling it up inside would be considered good psychological advice. Although Job experienced the deepest anguish of soul, he wasn't resentful. He did not have to worry about dealing with the problem of anger because he recognized that the central issue in life was trust — utter, simple, childlike dependency on God: "Though he slay me, yet will I trust Him." Since he was not dependent on anything other than God, he never became angry and hence never suffered from depression.

The core problem with the advice to express anger as a cure for depression was unwittingly pinpointed by Job's wife. Recognizing that God is sovereign, she realized that God is finally above and behind all that happens, including Satan's activity (and of course all of the work which he energizes like adultery, insults, a snub from someone in church). She encouraged Job to express anger and correctly assumed that ultimately anger over personal hurt or loss is always directed at God, the One who allowed all these horrible things to happen. Her words "Curse God and die" reflect the basic error with the advice to let the anger come pouring out. The anger is finally anger toward God for allowing this to happen to me. It will not do to say (as I have heard so often), "I'm not mad at God; I'm just good and mad at my husband for the way he treats me." God is where the buck-passing ends. Because He is sovereign, I must either thank Him or blame Him for what happens to me. If I could express anger at the sin of another rejecting me *without being personally threatened or hurt by the sin*, the anger would be righteous. But, by definition, the depressed person already has taken it personally (i.e "he doesn't love me and that makes me mad because I need his love," or my children, or my money, or whatever).

Although it would have required the kind of faith which moves mountains for Job to say "thank You" in the middle of his problems, I rather suspect that Job could easily thank God for it all as he contemplated in retrospect the marvelous loving purpose behind all his problems. The Book of Job is a vivid illustration of the truth of Romans 8:28: "And we know that all things work together for good to them that love God, to them who are the called according to his purpose." What is His purpose? I was chosen in Him before the foundation of the world to be holy and without blame (Eph. 1:4). And now, with the promises of God and the illustration of those promises before me in Scripture, I am to walk by faith and to thank God for every trial that comes up in my life, including those painful moments when people I love reject me. I can do it only by rigidly limiting my ultimate dependency to God.

Restricting dependency to God does not, however, minimize the importance and desirability of human relationships. It is right and normal to derive a wonderful sense of security from the love and fellowship of a spouse, of friends, of brothers and sisters in Christ. When God blesses me with the love of other people, I am to respond gratefully by enjoying their love and basking in the security it brings. But I am to recognize that my deepest care need for security is now being met and always will be met by an eternal, unchanging God of love. If loved ones turn on me, if I am placed in a situation where warm fellowship is unavailable, I am to aggressively believe that the biblical route to meeting security needs is to recognize that the sovereign God of the universe loves me. He is all that I need because He will arrange my world down to every minute detail (to believe that requires belief in a big God) in such a way that all my most basic needs will be met if I trust Him. Therefore, whatever happens to me, whether insults, loss of love, rejection, snubbing, not being invited to a certain social gathering, I am to respond with the rational, trusting response of thanksgiving.

Most of us do however "automatically" respond with anger to frustrating or painful circumstances. I am not suggesting that we repress our anger, pretend it doesn't exist, and force the words "Thank You, Lord" in an effort to prove how much we trust Him. So often people disguise resentment because they regard such feelings as unbecoming to a Christian. They are, but hiding them only compounds the problem. There is a difference between personally owning and acknowledging anger and freely venting it in an angry attack. The former is necessary. The latter is sinful. The depressed person should deal with his anger not by or resentfully attacking the source of hurt pain but (after fully acknowledging the felt anger and confessing it as the sin of misplaced dependency) by thanking God for the event which triggered his anger, believing that God is lovingly providing in every circumstance exactly what is best for my spiritual growth in becoming more like Jesus. Curse God and die? Continue to depend on others for security needs? Deal with your hurt by expressing your anger in open attack? Never really become secure in God's love, die as a person, remain unloved? No! Don't curse God and die. Thank God and live. Rest in the security of God's sovereign love. Be deeply secure as a person who thoroughly depends on God alone, trusting Him though he slay you. He always desires our best. Thank God and live the full, rich, personally satisfied life of one whose deep personal needs for security are met in the person of Jesus Christ.

Let me illustrate the point with a rather trivial personal incident. About a year ago, our family went on a week-end trip to Disney World. We packed the car, stopped at the orange groves to purchase fresh Florida orange juice, and began our three-and-a-half-hour journey in the highest of spirits. Our two boys (at that time three and five years old) were restlessly excited, my wife was smiling, and I was glowing inside with the anticipation of a fun family outing. Fifteen minutes away from home, we had a flat tire. In what is hopefully becoming less typical fashion, I responded with furious impatience, angrily pulling the car to the side of the turnpike, slamming the door as I got out, then jerking up the trunk to get the jack. My wife quickly poured a cup of cool orange juice for me in an effort to lower my emotional temperature. With a scowl, I gulped the juice and remained at boiling level. Then it hit me. I was not at that moment loving my wife as Christ loved the Church (or even coming close), nor was I at that moment bringing up my children in the nurture and admonition of the Lord. I was guilty of committing grievous sins which I had often counseled and preached against. And yet, even with this realization, I felt trapped by my anger. My problem was not so much the direction of my anger as it was the presence of anger. I was, in plain terms, mad about what happened. I was not getting my way. Expressing my irritation in "healthy, acceptable ways" did not seem to be the solution. Getting it out of my system was the goal, but shouting, kicking the tire, and slamming the trunk down did not seem to move me toward that goal at all. In fact, it tended to have quite the opposite effect. Forcing a smile, another alternative, seemed at worst impossible and at best hypocritical. I wanted to rid myself of my anger and to enjoy a deep, real, inner calm. But how to do it!

The words of Paul in Ephesians 5:20 floated into my consciousness: "Giving thanks always for *all* things." For a flat tire? But I do not enjoy flat tires and can see no advantage to having one. As a matter of fact, I had discovered that my tire was ruined beyond repair. But it further occurred to me that the God who is sovereign and omnipotent could certainly have prevented that flat tire. It also dawned on me with a fresh intensity that this mighty God loves me with an everlasting and perfect love. If I really believed these things and set my mind to think on them (setting your *mind* on biblical truth in the middle of frustrating circumstances is most of the battle), then, believing that all things must work together for good if these things are so, I had a rational basis for giving thanks for the flat tire. I did not *feel* like giving thanks. But the *facts* supported the *behavior* of giving thanks as an expression of rational, logical faith. (Again, notice the order. Begin with the *facts*. By faith *act* on them. The *feelings* will come.)

I went on to consider (still standing by the side of a

broken-down car on the turnpike) the overwhelmingly comforting truth that nothing can ever happen to me that my mighty, loving Father does not permit. He who freely gave me His Son will not hold back any good thing, even a flat tire. In order to appreciate the kind of "good thing" that included flat tires, it became immediately apparent that my life must be thoroughly dedicated to God's purposes. Flat tires were by no means good if my priorities were self-determined goals, like arriving at Disney World by such and such a time with a certain sum in my wallet. This observation suggested a general principle: whenever I have difficulty in giving thanks for something which happens in my world, it is likely that my goal is at that moment something other than conformity to the image of Christ. If I have yielded to Christ every right to what I may desire and am fixing my will to live for His purpose (which brings me significance), I am in a position to rationally thank God for everything because I rest secure in the knowledge that whatever happens can be turned into a growth experience for me. Another principle becomes evident: It is not what happens to me that matters; it is how I respond to what happens. If I respond with anger because I mistakenly believe that my needs are threatened or because my goals are self-determined, I run the risk of depression or resentment. If I respond with thanksgiving, meekly accepting all that God provides, I become more like the One who submitted to the hands of evil men because He delighted to do His Father's will, secure in a loving relationship that would never fail.

Although it is a wonderful, need-fulfilling truth that God loves us, it is difficult for each of us to lay hold of and appropriate the reality of an intangible, invisible Person's love. Jesus commanded us to love one another (John 15:12), to exhibit a true sense of community and oneness. Entering into the fullness of God's love is a growth process which God intends should be stimulated and nurtured in the loving fellowship of the local church. I am certainly not suggesting that since God loves me, I can become a social isolate without losing something wonderful. In one sense, we do need each other. In my own personal life, I find Christian fellowship (openly sharing with other Christians in Christ-centered conversation, sharing fun times, problems, new insights from Scripture) to be a vital source of encouragement. Do I need it? Yes, and therefore God has provided it. Should it ever be unavailable to me, I believe (although much grace would be necessary to implement this belief) Christ alone would be entirely sufficient for meeting my personal needs and to thus maintain my psychological integrity.

We are not to assume that because God's love is sufficient we are free from the responsibility to sacrificially and genuinely love each other. Quite the opposite. If I have been saved by His grace, it now is my privilege and responsibility to be a vehicle through which God can show His love for you. Churches often are such cold places. Warmth is limited to a locked-in smile and a "How are you today?" God never intended it to be so. People need love. Christ loves people. And He has designed the loving fellowship of believers to be the visible means of demonstrating His love to each other and to the world. As with significance needs, the local Christian community is God's primary instrument for meeting our security needs.

SUMMARY

If we are to understand the problems of people, we must look underneath the symptoms to the real personal needs of beings made in God's personal image. Basic to a proper understanding of people is the recognition that people need to regard themselves as worthwhile. In order to do so, we need to possess true significance and true security. Although most people in our world settle for a more or less satisfactory counterfeit basis for meeting these needs, they can ultimately and fully be met only in

Jesus Christ. The critical necessity is to regard this truth not as mere religious talk but as an urgent reality which makes an overwhelming difference in whether people are empty or filled, discontent or deeply satisfied, and then to develop the resources of the local church (exercise of gift and true fellowship) in responding to those needs.

7

Where Problems Start

ONE OF THE MOST debated issues in psychology concerns the role of thinking in the determination of behavior. Everyone seems to agree that people think and that somehow what they think is important, but different views abound of just how important thinking is and what causes people to think in specific ways. Let me justify the following semitechnical discussion of thinking (the word "perception" may be a more accurate term for what I am discussing) by asserting that I believe Scripture teaches that the starting point of all nonorganically caused emotional problems is a thinking problem, a wrong belief about how personal needs can be met. To properly understand the problems that people get themselves into, it is imperative that I develop some ideas about how people think.

Freud talked about primary process thinking. He was referring to the kind of thinking that conformed to the pleasure principle (experience pleasure at any cost) with no regard for the reality principle (what really is). If mother's breast is denied the infant, secondary process or realistic thinking would admit the delay, then attempt to shorten it or, if that were not possible, to accept it. Primary process thinking might lead to the hallucinated experience of enjoying what was really not there. Continued primary process thinking leads a person into his own private, nonreal world where gratification believed to be unavailable in reality is available on demand through fantasy. The element which I want to underline here is the notion that people are capable of trying to meet their needs in nonrational ways. Their thought worlds begin to include beliefs and ideas not bound by reality which they perceive will lead to need satisfaction.

Rogers took us ten steps backward by minimizing what a person thinks and focusing on his feelings. The phrase "emotional problem" reflects this emphasis on the feeling world of a person. Rogers does not believe that in order to help a troubled person one need do more than help a person assimilate his feelings (and he means literal visceral reactions, not cognitions). Whenever untrained, well-meaning people try to counsel, the first thing they do is ask someone, "How do you feel?" The question is all right but what do you do with the answer, "I feel lousy"? Rogerian types would respond with "You feel pretty low today." When the client then offers, "Yes, I really do. Can you help me?" the consistent mirroring counselor might reply, "You hope that I can be of help to you." I know of one dyed-in-the-wool Rogerian who in his role as academic advisor to graduate students has been known to respond to an advisee's question with "You're concerned about what courses to take to meet graduation requirements."

I strongly object to counselors who in the name of Scripture deny Rogers any hearing whatsoever. There is nothing wrong and sometimes everything right with sensitively and warmly reflecting a client's feelings in an attempt to understand him and (often just as important) to help him feel understood. The problem with Rogers is less with what he does and more with what he does not do. When I take my car to the mechanic and tell him my brakes do not hold, I suppose I would be pleasantly surprised if he said, "Hey, that's too bad. I'll bet that really concerns you." If, when I ask him to fix it, he warmly puts his hand on my shoulder, smiles, and replies, "You really feel anxious to have this fixed," I suppose my mood would turn from pleasant surprise to frustrated disbelief. I need his conceptual understanding of the problem and his resultant skill in repairing my brakes. His sympathy is appreciated but it is not enough. Why? Because the car is built according to a rational plan (although lifting one's hood tends to cast suspicion upon this assumption) and repairing it demands an intelligent understanding of that plan.

Now it is similarly clear that most things are the product of design or at least function according to a certain (though perhaps unspecified) regularity. Things do not seem to just randomly happen. When I have a pain in my chest, I assume it is not a random occurrence with neither cause nor solution. My doctor may not be able to diagnose the cause or he may fail in suggesting a solution but he (and all of medical science) assumes that there is a cause. Francis Schaeffer has pointed out that modern science was founded on the assumption that there is a discernable lawfulness and predictability in nature. I want more than my doctor's sympathy. I want him to identify the real cause of my problem and logically and scientifically predict (on the basis of previously observed regularity) what treatment will work. I do not assume (no one does) that my physical symptom is a random, chance occurrence.

There is no a priori reason whatever to suppose that psychological symptoms (maladaptive behavior, irrational fears, etc.) operate any less according to design than do physical symptoms. At some point a counselor needs to provide information on the rules which govern effective psychological living. But Rogers would have us encourage patients to move in whatever direction their "gut feelings" lead them. To assume, as Rogerians do, that there are no external laws which are universally applicable and which people must therefore obey if they are to enjoy personal (as opposed to physical) health requires that one single out personal functioning as totally different from everything else in nature. The point I wish to emphasize is that it is reasonable to assume that there is an external true reality which people must know and to which they must conform if they are to experience effective psychological functioning.

Let me restate the two points developed so far. First, people are capable of leaving reality behind in their efforts to meet personal needs. Second, there is a definite reality which does exist to which people must conform if they are to really meet their needs.

The next observation to be made involves a discussion of how thinking influences how we feel and what we do. Radical behaviorists empty thinking of any substance and speak strictly in terms of its external stimulus and external response. As you will recall from the third chapter, Skinner teaches that man is emotionally and rationally a zero, that nothing of any causal significance occurs inside the minds of people. He holds that what a person does can be totally accounted for by the forces (and history of forces) impinging upon that person. In a fascinating review of experiments, Don Dulany has gathered evidence that how a person interprets his world, what he believes to be in his world and what values he attaches to the various elements in his world influence and in fact control his behavior. He has systematized his thinking in what he calls the theory of propositional control. The propositions a person entertains in his mind, i.e. the sentences he speaks to himself, directly control what he eventually does. Albert Ellis has taken the argument a step further and asserts that not only do a person's internal sentences (which is really what thinking amounts to) control behavior but they also control a person's feelings. How a person evaluates a given event (that is terrible, this is nice, etc.) determines how a person will emotionally respond to that event. For example, if a loved one (Person A) dies, the living one (Person B) grieves. What causes the grief? Most would quickly say, "Why, the death of Person A made Person B unhappy." Suppose this same person died but Person B despised Person A. Now the same event (death of Person A) occasions a response of positive feelings, because Person B evaluates (says different things to himself) the event differently. In other words, the event does not control the feeling; the evaluation of the event controls it. Ellis calls this the A-B-C Theory of emotion: A (what happens to you) does not control C (how you feel); B (what you say to yourself about A) is in fact directly responsible for C (how you feel).

Although the arguments continue unabated, there is plenty of psychological evidence to support this third point I wish to make: how a person thinks has a great deal to do with what a person does and how a person feels.

Scripture, the Christian's final authority, supports the belief that psychologists are right when they emphasize the importance of thinking. "As a man thinketh. . . , so is he" (Prov. 23:7). In Romans 12:2 Paul beseeches us to not be conformed to this world (a false, untrue reality) but to be transformed by the renewing of our mind. Notice what this implies. (1) It is possible to believe in my thought-life a false reality. (2) There is a true reality to which I should conform. (3) If I am to order my life correctly before God it is necessary to think correct thoughts. In Ephesians 4:17 Paul writes: "This I say therefore, and testify in the Lord, that ye henceforth walk not as other Gentiles walk, in the vanity of their mind." He adds in verse 18 that their understanding is darkened. Wrong thinking leads to wrong walking (behaving and feeling). Scripture abounds with reference to the importance of right thinking. Apparently then, what we think is terribly important.

Let me summarize what has been said so far but I'll reverse the order of the points into a more logical one.

(1) What I think has a definite bearing on what I do and on what I feel.

(2) There is a true reality which I must be aware of (think about, believe) and behaviorally conform to if I am to enjoy a sense of personal well-being and an effective life.

(3) It is possible to believe something untrue and therefore to behave and to feel in ways that will result in my needs not being met.

The theme of this chapter can be stated in a sentence. Personal problems begin with a wrong belief which leads to behaviors and feelings which deny us the satisfaction of our deep personal needs. Think about the temptation of Eve. God had said that a certain behavior was prohibited. Picture a circle and call it the world which God had designed for Eve. Eating of the forbidden tree was an act outside the circle. The essence of Satan's temptation was to encourage Eve to say untrue sentences to herself, to believe something false: "My personal needs can be better met, I will be more worthwhile, if I go outside of God's circle." Until she actually ate of the forbidden tree, she would naturally resent the limits of the circle because she believed her needs could better be met outside the circle. And so she experienced the problem of resentment. As soon as she left the circle of obedience (which her wrong thinking led her to do), she offended the standards of a holy God who had claim to her obedience and so experienced the problem of guilt.

The problems of *resentment, guilt* and *anxiety* seem to be the three central underlying disorders in all personal problems and they exist because we think incorrect thoughts. (See Diagram 1 on page 82.) We believe that what God has provided is not best, whether it is harsh parents, a cold wife, an unloving husband, physical illness, whatever. We *resent* what God has given. When we disobey God in order to seize what He has disallowed (divorcing a disagreeable spouse), we are in a condition of *guilt*. When things in our lives are going our way and we are *depending* on them for our happiness, we worry that tomorrow things may take a turn for the worse and so we suffer from *anxiety*. It all begins with wrong thinking about how our personal needs are best met. We believe that to be happy our lives must be arranged in a certain way, we need certain things, and we insist on having them. We fail to trust our loving, infinite God to meet our needs.

The initial task of the biblical counselor is to recognize the basic personal needs of people (significance and security) and to identify the wrong thinking about how to meet those needs which has led to either sinful behavior (the problem then is guilt), or sinful feelings (resentment or anxiety). The human personality cannot function smoothly when guilt, resentment, or anxiety are present. To lastingly rid the person of these problems, the incorrect thought processes which occasioned the problem, thoughts which conformed to a wrong view of how to meet personal needs, must be identified and corrected. And accomplishing that is the substantial part of the counseling enterprise.

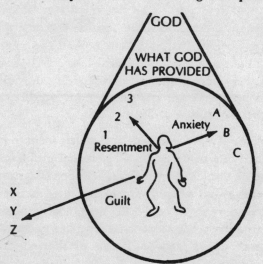

Diagram 1: **The Three Roots of Emotional Problems**

The circle represents the world in which I live. I like B (e.g. money) but I am depending on having it to meet my needs. Because I cannot fully control whether I will have B tomorrow I am *anxious*. I hate #2 (e.g. unloving husband), and I refuse to accept it as God's loving provision because I wrongly believe I need something else in order to be worthwhile. Therefore I am *resentful*. I believe I need Y (e.g. another woman), and so I step outside the circle of God's provision to get it. I am then *guilty*. The basic cure is learning to be content in whatever circle is mine.

Weaving Tangled Webs

THUS FAR I HAVE developed the notion that people have needs and I have discussed a few basic concepts about thinking. My purpose in this chapter is to see how a counselor, armed with these fundamental ideas, can understand the confusing array of problems confronting him in his office.

A mother laments: "I love my daughter but I lose my patience with her. It gets so bad sometimes I really hit her hard in anger. I know it's wrong. My pastor has already told me that and insisted that I stop it. But I still do it. I feel terrible about it." A biblical counselor would begin by saying to himself as he listens to the distraught mother: "She has a deep need to regard herself as worthwhile. In order to meet that need, she must meet the two sub-needs of significance and security. Somehow she is thinking wrong about how to meet those needs; she is depending on the wrong things. I know all that. So now what do I do?" The task of this chapter is to fill in the considerable gap between the premise and the problem. Filling in the gap requires first some discussion of early childhood development. Amid the enchantment with the "radical now" which regards an excursion into developmental history as no more necessary (but sometimes almost as long) as the forty years' wilderness wandering, investigating the genetic components of personal problems may seem contrary to a biblical model. Most of us are thoroughly disillusioned with traditional therapy's long journey into childhood, searching for the unconscious infantile fixation which holds the key to our adult troubles. The behaviorists, Gestaltists, reality therapists, Rogerians, existentialists, Mowrerians, nouthetic counselors, and others have convincingly argued against the orthodox psychoanalytical thesis that without a detailed study of historical content (assumed to be charged with negative emotion and repressed in the unconscious), no significant personality changes can take place. Scripture abounds with the liberating truth that we are not slaves to our past; we are slaves to Christ who has freed us from the chains of a sinful nature. The Lord is wonderfully capable of revolutionizing lives. He took impetuous, aggressive Peter and transformed him (without, as far as we know, analyzing his childhood) into the still assertive but now patient fatherly type evidenced in his two epistles. The apostle John was another remarkable transformation: from a vengeful (Luke 9:54), exclusive (Luke 9:49), and ambitious (Matt. 20:21) man he was transformed into the gentle apostle of love. A personality change was accomplished by his spending time with Jesus. The list of sinful personality patterns recorded in 1 Corinthians 6:9, 10 is long and depressing. Paul remarks, "and such *were* some of you" — past tense. Those people had changed. How? By coming to the Savior and finding His power to conform to His image. Countless testimonies could be given by drunks, liars, cheats, hot-tempered husbands, etc., affirming the reality of God's magnificent power to profoundly change a personality.

A biblical counselor will enter into counseling with a confident belief in these exciting truths. But he will want more. He will want to understand precisely what the problem is that is preventing his client from experiencing God's transforming power. He knows that transformation comes by renewing the mind, by thinking true thoughts which build upon the reality of God. He will need to know exactly what the client is thinking that is getting him into trouble. And in order to understand what a client is thinking now, it is often helpful to understand how people learn to think specific thoughts about how their needs can be met. History becomes important when it contributes to our understanding of the present, or more exactly, of the present wrong thinking which is behind problem behaviors or feelings.

In the first few years of life, children develop a general impression of the world, particularly the world of people. People are nice. People hurt. People love. People ignore. As language develops, these inarticulate, generalized impressions are clothed with words and so develop thoughts or beliefs. The world is perceived in a rather global, undifferentiated way. All people tend to be seen as possessing similar attributes as the significant adults in a child's life. It is in this world of people as he perceives it that the growing child must learn some way to meet his deep needs for significance and security. Proverbs 22:15 teaches that foolishness is bound in the heart of a child. Children naturally will be looking for ways to meet their needs without turning to God. That is foolishness. There are no such ways. But children are foolish. There are none that seek after God, neither yours nor mine. Children assume the truth of Satan's lie to Eve that "you can better meet your needs on your own; determine your own course of action; look out for yourself; insist on having things your way if you want to be happy." The sin nature is having its death-producing effect in the minds of children from the moment of birth. The behavior of infants belies their thinking: "I will be satisfied only if you snap to whenever I holler." As the infant becomes a toddler and then a school-age youngster, his mind is forming assumptions about how he can best meet his needs for regarding himself as worthwhile: "If I have the neatest bike on the block, if I can get Mom to notice me more than she does my brother, if I can win the game of checkers," etc. It seems to be the case that as time goes by every person develops a general working belief which pretty well governs all his behavior. Adler calls this a working or guiding fiction, a belief about how best to compensate for felt inferiority, a belief that influences much of what I do or do not do. Tim LaHaye has written interesting material on different temperaments, reviving the Hippocratic notion that each of us has a relatively fixed personality style. Most parents would agree that regardless of similarity in child training procedures, children develop unique, highly individualized personalities. Without wanting to enter the nature-nurture debate, I wonder if part of the explanation for different styles of personality lies in an under-standing of (1) how a child perceives his world and (2) what he believes is the best way to operate in this world to get his needs met. A single experience of painful trauma may teach a sensitive child that "people hurt." The best way to move in a world full of hurting people is with caution. As a result of never warmly and openly relating to others, he never experiences the uplifting joys of interpersonal care and intimacy. Perhaps this is one kind of background that produces the moody, listless melancholic which LaHaye describes.

The two critical points to understand are, first, that each of us tends to unconsciously perceive the world of people (at least the world of people close to us) in a rather stereotyped fashion which was learned in childhood, and, second, we entertain a basic belief about what pattern of behavior is appropriate in our world to meet our personal needs. To the degree that that belief is in error we will experience problems in living.

To illustrate this thinking, let me return to the mother who loses control over her daughter. The biblical counselor knows before she walks into his office that she has deep personal needs, that they probably are not very well met (very few come to a counselor to tell him how fulfilled they are), and that she must therefore be operating according to wrong assumptions about how those needs can be met. Simple, direct questions growing out of the counselor's preliminary understanding might reveal the following pertinent information. Her mother was a cold, unloving, undemonstrative type woman. Her dad was Mr. Neutral and rarely home. A fairly obvious conclusion from these few facts would be that her early world was rather unrewarding.

The next line of questioning would concern those patterns of behavior a child in that world might believe to be most effective in meeting her needs. As she grows up, it might be discovered that the only things she ever received attention for involved her ability to competently manage club activities, to organize neighborhood parties, to diligently study and earn good grades. And so she comes to believe, "I will regard myself as worthwhile if I can handle things because the only thing which ever earned any recognition at all from my parents was competent management." She later gets married, still holding on to her faulty assumption. Perhaps she chooses a rather docile man she believes she can handle. For a time she seems to successfully handle her marriage and is feeling relatively secure, although without Christ's unconditional love filling her heart she becomes aware of a nagging pressure to keep on demonstrating competence in order to maintain her security. And then a daughter comes along. The infant cuddles in mother's arms, smiles more for mother (the source of food) than for anyone else, and mother is feeling wonderfully competent in her new role and happily secure.

As a few years pass by, mother notices more and more disconcerting behavior on her daughter's part. She does not mind as well as she should. In a number of ways, she does not behave as mother really wants her to. Perhaps dad unhelpfully and unwittingly comments that daughter seems to be out of control or criticizes something mother does. Mother feels threatened. She overreacts with panic, frustration, near hysteria. What is at stake: *mother's need for security*. Every instance of misbehavior comes to be seen as a challenge to mother's competence and since her security is wrapped up in her competence, her deepest personal needs become involved. All this because of a wrong and foolish belief about how to be secure. And so she redoubles her efforts to control her daughter. Predictably the daughter resists the added pressure more and more, becoming increasingly unmanageable. Mother starts to come apart at the seams and turns into a hysterical woman, the very opposite of the calm, competent person she set out to be. In her frustration, she angrily strikes out at the obstacle to her need fulfillment, her unruly daughter, and so the problem develops.

Mowrer speaks of the "neurotic paradox." Why do people behave in ways that obviously are ineffective in producing the results they want? The answer I believe is clear: because they are believing a lie, a wrong assumption about how to meet their needs, and are behaving consistently with that assumption. Since their psychological existence (regarding themselves as worthwhile) is at stake, they will unrelentingly follow their belief. But because they are wrong in their thinking, their behavior will *not* lead to need satisfaction.

What might the biblical counselor tell the frustrated mother? "You need to feel secure. You have learned that the way to feel secure is to manage things effectively, thus displaying your competence and earning recognition. This belief first of all is simply incorrect, and we will discuss this later. Second, your belief is ineffective. It is leading you to efforts to control your daughter. Now whose needs are you trying to meet when you discipline or advise your daughter? Her needs or yours? Obviously yours. Therefore your daughter feels used by you and in fact she is. She feels that you are wanting her to be good not for her sake but for yours. And that is contributing to *her* feeling insecure. She is learning to handle her insecurity by fighting you, by not being sucked into a relationship where she is reduced to a thing and not a person. Can you therefore see how operating according to your belief is simply ineffective in ever getting your daughter to mind? But seeing that still leaves us with a problem — if your way of meeting your security needs is ineffective, how can they be met? And the answer depends upon the first observation I made— that your belief is simply incorrect.   One does *not* achieve security by being a successfully controlling person."

At that point a discussion of the real need for *unconditional* love is in order, followed by a presentation of the gospel of love in Jesus Christ. I might mention that it is all right to tell a client in teaching form what is wrong. There are however two dangers in a mini-lecture: (1) the client might tune you out and let his attention drift elsewhere and (2) the effect of hearing truth from another is less than seeing truth for yourself. Sometimes a Socratic method of leading the client to state the right conclusions has more impact on the client. Matters of technique need to be thoroughly discussed elsewhere.

There are as many subtle variations of wrong beliefs as there are people. And yet the basic format is invariant. "I believe that I will feel significant (or secure) if . . . ." When the counselor is able to finish the sentence, he will have an explanation of the presenting problem of the client.

Let me offer another illustration of how tangled webs are woven with the twine of mistaken beliefs. (Details of case studies are altered enough to prevent identification. As you read these illustrations, be assured that I am not referring to whoever you think I am.) A young man, thirty-three years old, consulted me concerning a serious problem with chronic lying. From a biblical viewpoint, I must label lying a sin and not a symptom of mental illness for which my patient is not responsible. It does not follow that counseling becomes a process of merely rebuking the sin and exhorting honesty. Of course both those elements would be included in any counseling effort based on Scripture. It is interesting to notice that just before Paul exhorts us to put on the new man and to put off lying (Eph. 4:24, 25), he speaks of the need to be renewed in the spirit of our minds. A biblical counselor will want to get into his client's mind, determine what he is thinking that is leading to trouble. If your personality is aggressive enough and forceful enough you may be able to rebuke the sin with sufficient strength to produce a marked decrease in lying behavior. But you have not solved the problem. The wrong thinking remains unchanged.

A brief history obtained from the client included the following pertinent information: he was the youngest of five children, his dad was the dominant figure at home but he remembered no warm interaction with him. His mother was a quiet, gentle person who loved her son dearly. Perhaps she pampered her youngest a little, regarding him as her "special" child. His father's perfectionistic standards (and severe discipline for imperfection) combined with his mother's attitude that "my little Johnny wouldn't do anything wrong" presented him with a world where recognition and approval depended on flawless conduct. If he erred, his dad punished him in a rage of anger and frustration. If his mother saw him misbehaving (and if the misbehavior was too obvious to permit her rationalizing that it was another's fault), she was transparently and painfully disappointed. His guiding belief became "I will be adequate if I am perfect. When I am not perfect, I can maintain a sense of adequacy by not admitting imperfection and thus not incurring angry rejection or a look of grieved disappointment."

Because of his wrong belief, this man now experienced the problem of *guilt*. He had to lie to protect his adequacy and lying is outside the circle of the life God has planned. He also had the problem of *resentment*, particularly toward himself for not being perfect. Rather than accepting himself as a sinner who, in spite of his sins, is loved by a merciful, loving God, he came to deeply hate any signs of imperfection because they were a threat to his adequacy. *Anxiety* was also a problem. He knew he was imperfect and he resented it; he was guilty of lying to hide his blemished behavior. He continually feared that he would be found out, so he experienced a deep, anxious uneasiness. Notice how a wrong, foolish belief created the three roots of personal problems: guilt, anxiety, resentment.

This sort of analysis is not meant to reduce the heinousness of sin by evoking sympathy for the mistreated sinner. It rather is an attempt to better elucidate the entire sin, to look beneath the tip of the iceberg — the lying — and to see its foundations — incorrect, sinful thinking. The diagnostic part of the counseling process uncovers the wrong beliefs supporting the sinful pattern of behavior. Treatment involves teaching right beliefs, exhorting right behavior consistent with right beliefs, and identifying the gratifying feelings which right living produces.

8

Weaving Tangled Webs Appendix

In brief, outline form, let me now sketch three more case studies. Read the *presenting problem*, the *assumptions*, and the *history*, then before reading the *root problem* and *observations*, see if you can complete the sentence for each patient "I will regard myself as worthwhile if . . . ." Try to identify a basis for resentment, anxiety, or guilt.

A. *Presenting Problem*: Marital conflict: broken-down communication.

Assumptions: Husband is not loving and wife is not submitting because neither believe that biblical roles would lead to fulfillment. Each is somehow trying to meet his/her needs through hostile, cold behavior. The core problem is wrong thinking.

History: Wife: raised by alcoholic father and domineering mother. Never knew security of a father's consistent love: he promised much and delivered little.

Husband: raised by strict, overly harsh father and weak, docile mother. Remembers being beaten severely (for minor misbehavior) in front of his buddies. Swore to himself, "I will never be controlled again by anyone as long as I live."

Root Problem:

Wife: WRONG BELIEF: I need to be shown the sensitive love I never had. If my husband does not do things for me, it means I am unloved and therefore worthless.

RESENTMENT: emotionally chained to her father because of strong grudge against him. Was compensating in the present for a past problem — holding on to past problem by resentment. Resented husband for any insensitive behavior which, according to the belief system, threatened her deepest personal needs.

Husband: WRONG BELIEF: I can regard myself as a man (independent, important, etc.) only if I never give in to someone else's demands.

ANXIETY: fear of being dominated.

RESENTMENT: against father for whipping and against wife for trying to control (asking for a kiss, etc.).

Both experienced guilt as they behaved consistently with their sinful beliefs. She continued to apply more pressure and became a frustrated manipulator. He resisted her demands by angrily withdrawing — eventually committed adultery to prove to himself he was not controlled by her.

Every conversation became an attempt to change the one to meet the other's needs. "You should be nicer to me." "You shouldn't try to control me."

Observations:

1. Non-Christian approach would provide some help; husband could see that being nice to wife did not mean being controlled but was rather a responsible, mature choice. Wife could be shown that his coldness was not a rejection of her but was rather a reaction to his own needs. By changing her approach (making no demands) he would be freed to be nice.

2. If such an approach worked, there still would be a real problem: she still was depending on him for security and he still

was not willing to submit to any authority. Wrong beliefs would continue to cause trouble whenever either would not get his/her way.

B. *Presenting Problem*: Teen-age rebellion: seventeen-year-old boy belligerent with parents, wants to leave home, quit school, get job and an apartment. Neither reasoning nor ordering has been helpful.

Assumptions: Boy striving for significance with this sinful (disobedient) behavior because of wrong thinking.

History: Father capable, loving, head of house; mother is kind, gentle, good. Parents both overprotective of client (youngest of four). Helped him make all his decisions. Client trusted Christ at age twelve — "on fire" for Lord from then until soon after sixteenth birthday. Rebellion grew gradually over last fourteen months to present proportions.

Root Problem:

WRONG BELIEF: In order to be significant, to respect myself, I've got to be my own person, which for me means making my own decisions rather than following dad's leadership.

RESENTMENT: Against dad for offering so much (good) advice.

GUILT: Acting sinfully toward parents. Tried several times to change but became angry every time dad gave more advice (threatened his significance).

His behavior was quite consistent with his beliefs. Doing what dad did not suggest established his significance according to his belief.

Observations: Accepting parents as God's agents to direct him into a significant life demanded a different criterion for significance: significance comes from doing God's will.

C. *Presenting Problem*: Depression: twenty-three-year-old girl: "I hate myself, how I look, my personality, everything." Has expressed suicidal thoughts.

101

Assumptions: She feels unloved as she is. Has retreated into "no-contact" depression, little agitation, blah, perfunctory living; therefore one must question whether her symptoms are really an effort to get attention or perhaps are more a rational response of despair to a sense of inevitable worthlessness.

Note on suicide: When client is still agitated and upset, he hasn't given up. Suicide attempt, if made, will most likely be manipulative gesture.

When client becomes "merely quiet," cooperatively docile, risk is much higher because such behavior reflects a no-hope attitude. These folks desperately need the biblical message of hope (1 Cor. 10:13).

History: "Ugly duckling" since birth: problems with skin, teeth, eyes, figure, hair. Two siblings, each normally attractive. Rejection by peers (comments, jokes, etc.) taught her that she was unacceptable. Parents' genuine acceptance was seen by her as forced, not real. Had been slipping slowly into deeper and deeper depression; no signs of snapping out of it, as parents had hoped.

Root Problem:

WRONG BELIEF: In order to be accepted by anyone, I need to be more acceptable. I will be secure only if accepted on my personal merits. Because I have so many demerits, I will never be secure. There is no hope of having my needs met: I am personally dead.

RESENTMENT: Against peers for their rejection; against parents for their "forced" love; most of all, against her appearance — learned to hate herself.

Observations:

1. Apart from Christianity, encouragements to "accept yourself" are really humanistic hot air. "You're as good as anyone else." Not as far as getting acceptance goes. "Externals don't matter, it's inner beauty that counts." Helpful idea but does not

change the fact that unfortunate externals do produce a painful reaction from others.

2. Only the recognition that loving God is in control can provide security. Christianity provides rational basis for saying "thank you" for all the negatives; provides genuine self-acceptance.

9

Hold Your Client
Responsible: For What?

In RECENT YEARS, THE unifying theme of a variety of new approaches to counseling has been a strong emphasis on personal responsibility. William Glasser devotes the opening chapter of *Reality Therapy* to a repudiation of the Freudian concept of determinism. Freud teaches that people are helplessly driven by intrapsychic forces set in motion by the experiences of early childhood. It is right and proper therefore, according to Freud, to speak of the affliction of mental illness, a psychological disorder for which the sufferer bears no responsibility. The job of the therapist is to sympathetically accept his inappropriate behavior as the necessary result of forces beyond the client's control and to provide new influences which will negate the ill effects of the old ones. The net effect of this thinking is the removal of personal responsibility for behavior. Skinner is just as much (and sometimes more explicitly) a thoroughgoing naturalistic determinist as Freud. Rather than shifting responsibility from the person to his internal environment, he locates the source of all control in the external environment. In either case, man is stripped of the dignity of independent movement and so cannot logically be held responsible for his behavior.

In reaction to this sort of thinking, Glasser leads the cry of a few secular psychologists for a renewed awareness of the importance of personal responsibility. Hold your patient responsible for what he does. Point out alternatives, help him evaluate their relative merits, then lay the burden for choosing what course to follow squarely on the client. Tell a nagging wife to stop nagging and a critical husband to stop criticizing; tell a fearful neurotic to stop being controlled by his fears and to do what he fears doing.

Christians who have spoken up on the side of responsibility need to be aware of a serious but subtle danger in such thinking. To hold a shrewish wife responsible to speak pleasantly and to do nice things, may easily promote effort in the power of the flesh. "I've got to stop nagging. I'll try real hard this week to be the gracious wife God wants me to be." Some Christians would suggest that rather than trying so hard she should "let go and let God." Does that mean that there is no place for effort on our part? If that is the case, then we have returned to a position of non-responsibility. If I cannot curb my tongue in my strength, then perhaps I am not responsible to try. And yet most Christians, while agreeing on the one hand that man is helpless, on the other hand hold him responsible. In order to resolve this apparent dilemma, we need to precisely define the sphere of responsibility. Biblical counselors need to hold their clients responsible only for what they can control. To do otherwise is to promote discouragement.

Let me pick up the thread from the last chapter. The client now has been shown what his needs are. His mistaken beliefs about how he can meet his needs have carefully been traced from their inception to their present form. The correct answer to the fundamentally important question "On what basis can I legitimately regard myself as worthwhile, both significant and secure?" has been presented (see chapters 4 and 5). The client has been helped to see how his sinful pattern of behavior and his emotional problems have stemmed from his wrong thinking. A course of action consistent with right thinking and designed to promote effective interaction with his world has been precisely identified.

What is the next step in counseling? Should the client at this point be told that he is responsible to behave in God-pleasing ways and that because he is a Christian (assuming he really is) he has all the power he needs to do so through the indwelling Spirit? Should plans be made, assignments be given, steps be outlined? In Ephesians 4 Paul tells us to renew our minds and then to put on the new man, or, in other words, clear up our thinking, then shape up our behavior. The order seems to be think right, then live right. Yet it has been my experience in counseling to watch a person identify his wrong beliefs, consciously change them to correct ones, and then to fail in seemingly sincere efforts to live changed lives. Something is missing. The missing step between thinking right and acting right is supplied when we understand the primary sphere of man's responsibility.

Throughout Scripture, life in our sin-stained world always is preceded by death.

"Except a corn of wheat fall into the ground and die, it abideth alone: but if it *die*, it bringeth forth much fruit (a changed life?)" (John 12:24).

"Therefore we are buried with him by baptism into death: that like as Christ was raised up from the dead by the glory of the Father, even so we also should walk in newness of *life*. For if we have been planted together in the likeness of his *death*, we shall be also in the likeness of his *resurrection*" (Rom. 6:4, 5).

"Now if we be *dead* with Christ, we believe that we shall also *live* with him" (Rom. 6:8).

"Likewise reckon ye also yourselves to be *dead* indeed unto sin, but *alive* unto God through Jesus Christ our Lord" (Rom. 6:11). The order is clear and consistent: first death, then life. In some sense, when Christ died I died. Therefore I can live even as

107

He lives with sin's penalty paid. It is interesting to notice that the first exhortation in Romans occurs in Romans 6:11: "reckon ye also yourselves *dead*." Count it true. In verse 12 Paul seems to be saying that as we count ourselves really dead, we will implement this by *choosing not to sin*. Here is the core of the Christian's responsibility (and I believe the central element in overcoming temptation). When I am faced with a sinful pattern of thinking ("my significance needs can be met through recognition"), and I therefore am prompted to behave sinfully, I am to die to that sinful pattern experientially just as I already am dead to it positionally. I am to actualize in my immediate experience that which God says is true: I am dead to sin. In other words, I am to identify with Christ in His death by doing with sin exactly what He did with sin. Both the Father and the Son, in the events of the cross, shouted a thunderous *no* to sin. The Father turned His back on His lovely Son when Jesus was made sin for me. Christ freely submitted to His Father's will by allowing the soldiers to nail Him to the cross, agreeing with the Father that sin must be punished. By hanging on the cross, He was providing the basis for shouting an eternal no to sin.

God holds me responsible for shouting an equally thunderous no to sin in my life. In plain language, I am to decide, when faced with the possibility of yielding to sin, that I *will not do so* because I reject sin even as God does. That is my first responsibility in leading a changed life: willing not to sin existentially, moment by moment, when the urge is there, and then claiming the life of Christ as the resource for overcoming temptation. The actual act of resisting often will involve what I subjectively feel as teeth-gritting effort. I will be aware of the struggle of moving against a powerful tide. I will be swimming upstream and my arms will get tired. Victory depends upon first *deciding* not to sin, deciding to swim upstream, against the current, and second, *believing* that God's power is sufficient to resist the seemingly overwhelming rush of internal feelings and urges.

Understanding this, the biblical counselor will discuss the client's attitude toward the identified sin in his thoughts and actions. It is amazing to note the casualness with which so many react to acknowledged personal sin. If beneath our consciously sincere efforts to change our behavior, we are really saying to ourselves "Y'know, I really shouldn't sin; I guess I had better try not to do it anymore," there will never be lasting change. There has been no experienced death, therefore there can be no experienced life. Another common attitude is "I know I'm wrong but so is he. My sin is no worse than his;" or perhaps, "Sure my sin is wrong, but what do you expect? Look what I'm going through. Could you make it through this without resentment or feeling sorry for yourself?" Whatever the attitude, without a decisive no to sin at the moment of temptation, without the present choice of *death* to wrong patterns, there will be no experience of present life in Christ, a life of victory and change.

Putting on the new man requires first putting off the old man by asserting with all our strength a decisive, deliberate no to sin. And then we are to keep on saying no, every day, as long as we live, every moment of our lives. (Of course we will fail. We sometimes will say yes to sin. The wonder of the cross is its infinite efficacy in restoring me to fellowship no matter how often I sin.)

After counseling has identified wrong beliefs and taught right beliefs, the next step involves the client's *decision* to put off the practice of sin and to put on the practice of righteousness. Without this step, exhortations to change will produce surface, temporary results.

Let me illustrate the process. Some months ago I was flying from Detroit to Ft. Lauderdale. When the meal was served, I immediately noticed the chocolate eclair in the rear left corner of my tray. I hurried through the lukewarm, more or less palatable meal, in anticipation of the epicurean joys before me. When I was ready for the eclair, I noticed with dismay that I had emptied my coffee cup. I am one of those whose pleasure in eating sweet desserts is immeasurably enhanced by sipping hot, aromatic coffee. Picture my dilemma. The stewardess was busy and it appeared that I would have perhaps ten minutes wait before I could have more coffee. A space of approximately twelve inches separated my mouth from the eclair and I knew I should wait. My thinking was quite clear: greater pleasure would be mine if I waited the ten minutes. I had counseled myself to the point of identifying my need (pure sensual pleasure); I realized the incorrectness of my belief that my needs could better be met by immediate consumption.

The next step in my self-counseling was to hold myself responsible not to eat. And so I began reviewing the situation mentally. "Larry," I told myself, "you really ought to wait. It's the best way to meet your needs. You should be able to wait a mere ten minutes. You know it's best. Your beliefs are in order. So wait." Since I was thoroughly convinced by my arguments, I was chagrined to notice my hand grasping the fork and moving steadily toward the rear left corner of the tray. My consternation was mingled with a guilty pleasure shortly thereafter as I carefully savored the chocolate flavor which filled my mouth. Noticing that the single bite had reduced the size of the eclair by one third, I frantically returned to my internal debate. "Larry, you really blew it. Sure it was good, but there is no coffee to round out the pleasurable moment. Picture the joys of coffee and *wait, wait, wait.*"

Armed with a new resolve and feeling quite confident, I again noticed with alarm the movement of my fork-carrying hand. After my second third, it occurred to me that my rather trivial defeat paralleled the defeat of so many people who know to do right, who want to do right, and proceed to do wrong. I could not chalk up my defeat to lack of will power. If that were the reason, I was destined to continued defeat since I had no idea how to

110

quantitatively increase my will power. In reflecting on my dilemma, I was struck by what was the real lack. I had understood my needs, I was thinking right, and I earnestly wanted to do right, but I had never died to the eclair by saying "No, " by making a firm, conclusive, assertive, emphatic negative decision. *Underneath I was still entertaining the possibility of giving in!*

After checking to see that no one was either watching or within earshot, I glared steadfastly at the eclair, and quietly but most firmly said "No." The fruit of the victory that followed a few minutes later was a single mouthful of eclair with a sip of hot coffee both before and after.

The illustration is silly. The point is critical. Before embarking on a program of behavior change, secure a firm commitment to change based on a clear vote against sin. To state the whole matter simply and in more familiar language, repentance, a deliberate choice to turn around, based on a change of mind, must precede behavior change. It should go without saying among Christian counselors that part of my assertive rejection of sin would always include the specific confession of any known sin to the offended party: always to the Lord and often to a specific person against whom the sin was committed. Although I am presuming an awareness of the necessity of confession, perhaps some counselors could overlook the obvious. The biblical procedure for change is clear: confession and repentance. First acknowledge your sin before the cross of Christ, ask for forgiveness and restored fellowship. Then decisively turn from that sin, repent of it, aggressively decide to reject it as a life style, say no to sin. And then work out your salvation in the practice of righteousness, walking by choice in the good works to which we have been ordained.

Hold your client responsible: for what? For confessing his sin, for wilfully and firmly turning from it, and then for practicing the new behavior, believing that the indwelling Spirit will provide

111

all the needed strength. The sequence is critical. We can now add important detail to the sketch of the counseling process presented in chapter 4.

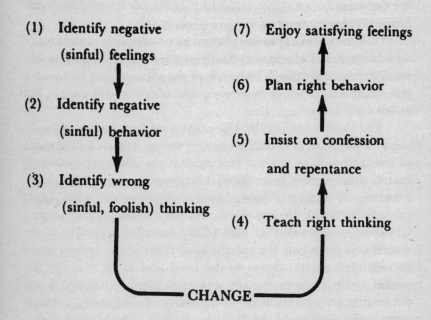

(1) Identify negative (sinful) feelings

(2) Identify negative (sinful) behavior

(3) Identify wrong (sinful, foolish) thinking

(4) Teach right thinking

(5) Insist on confession and repentance

(6) Plan right behavior

(7) Enjoy satisfying feelings

CHANGE

Let me illustrate briefly the importance of choosing not to sin. A married Christian man was plagued by strong homosexual urges. Every three or four weeks the urge became so strong he yielded and practiced homosexual behavior. Secular psychiatric efforts had traced the development of his aberrant sexual desire. As is often the case, insight did not produce change. He simply better understood himself as he continued to seek out a homosexual partner every three weeks. Pastoral counseling had included a strong denunciation of his behavior as sin, reminders that the indwelling Holy Spirit provided all the power he needed for resisting temptation, prayer, exhortations to stop, church disciplinary action — all to no avail. My patient reported that he would be encouraged after a prayer session with the elders, feel no urge for weeks, but then it would come back with increased intensity. When he tried to "let go and let God," his urges carried him to his homosexual partner. When he tried to resist the temptation himself, while repeating his firm belief that strength comes from God, the urges overwhelmed his strength and he succumbed again. Why was God not providing the needed strength? What was wrong?

In talking with him, it became clear that he was looking for victory from one of two sources: either the desire would be weakened or greater strength would be granted to resist the desire. Neither option depended on him at all. He was responsible for nothing. Underneath his failing behavior, he was rather passively saying "Lord, I really don't want to sin. Help me." Further discussion indicated that his whole life style was rather passive. He rarely took any bull by the horns. I pointed out that his responsibility was to aggressively and assertively *decide not to sin* now and also right at the point of temptation. Then trust God to work in him both to will and to do of His good pleasure. The power of the Holy Spirit was released in him when he firmly committed himself by choice to go God's way. The strength to resist was there in abundance. Victory depended on his assuming responsibility for what he could control: making a clear decision to obey God by not sinning.

10

The Mood and Goal
of Counseling

THE MOOD

I AM IMPRESSED WITH the fact that Paul seems to beseech more
than command. The New Testament is full of clear directions:
Don't commit adultery, don't lie, do bear each other's burdens,
give thanks for everything, don't gossip, etc. Paul typically beseeches us to conform to the pattern of Christ as described by
these instructions. In his farewell speech to the Ephesian elders,
Paul speaks of counseling the Ephesians with tears. One does not
get the impression that Paul harshly ordered people to shape up.
Some of the recent books on Christian counseling have been
interpreted by some to encourage an almost cold, impersonal
approach: "Look, here's what Scripture says. If you want it,
fine — it will work. If you don't, OK — have it your way."

C. S. Lewis, in *The Weight of Glory*, speaks of regarding no
man as a mere mortal. If we could now see the lowliest of persons
in their eternal state, we would either shrink with horror from the
embodiment of evil desolation or we would fall to our knees
inclined to worship one with the beauty of conformity to Christ.
When I see people as marvelous though fallen beings, my attitude

will shift from "take it or leave it" to "I long for you to take it; the joy available to you is your intended destiny." Although a biblical counselor will always hold people responsible and will never compromise scriptural principles, his approach, though often firm and tough, will never be harsh, cynical, sarcastic, or indifferent. It will be characterized by the gentle love of a High Priest who can be touched with the feelings of our infirmities. When a person is not willing to go God's way, but insists on hanging on to resentment, self-pity, and other sinful patterns, the counselor will confront directly but gently, firmly but warmly. If there is no response, the client may have to be told regretfully to come back when he is ready to do business with God.

People who are having problems are hurting. When the sorrow is the necessary result of obedience to God (such as the agony of Jesus in Gethsemane), loving support is appropriate. When sorrow is really a rebellion against God-appointed circumstances, loving confrontation is necessary.

THE GOAL

Psychotherapists used to insist that values had no place in their profession. For years it was assumed that professional counseling was a scientific enterprise akin to dentistry or surgery. Few Christians would insist that their dentist share their conservative evangelical beliefs. Most would easily select a highly skilled agnostic dentist over a run-of-the-mill Christian. If counseling is a technique governed entirely by scientific understanding, why should Christians concern themselves with finding a counselor who is a Christian? He would behave in much the same way that a non-Christian counselor would behave.

The parallel between dentistry and counseling breaks down immediately when one considers the goal of each discipline. Both professions seek to diagnose deviations from the norm of health and to restore the afflicted person to that norm as closely as possible. The essential question therefore becomes "What is health?" There would be little disagreement between a group of non-Christian dentists and a group of Christian dentists in defining a healthy mouth. Whatever difference there might be between these groups certainly would have nothing to do with their theology. But Christian and non-Christian psychologists may have significantly greater trouble reaching agreement on a definition of the healthy personality. What is considered healthy depends in large degree upon the value system of the diagnostician. To a secular counselor, a healthy adjustment to marital problems may be divorce. To a biblical counselor, remaining with a consistently disagreeable spouse may be evidence of obedience to God and the means of character growth. Secular counselors may promote adjustment to a homosexual life style by allaying guilt and promoting self-acceptance while a biblical counselor would insist upon confession of homosexual activity as sin and a commitment to forsake such immorality. I might mention that even Christian therapists sometimes lose sight of the goal of Christlikeness and cure one sin by promoting another.

I once heard a Christian psychiatrist report his successful treatment of a homosexual. A program of planned masturbation while looking at *Playboy* centerfolds (a standard behavior therapy technique) had increased heterosexual desire to the point where the unmarried patient was taking his girl friend to bed. His cure strikes me as no more worthy than teaching a bank robber the fine skills of embezzlement.

I recently counseled with a woman married to a strong aggressive male who asserted his headship. A secular psychologist had informed her that the husband was unmistakably chauvinistic and needed an updating of his views on marriage. Although it was apparent that the man was using his malehood as a tyrannical club, I thoroughly supported his role as head while rebuking his unbiblical lack of love. I exhorted the wife to submit to him as he

117

was, a suggestion directly contradicting my colleague's thinking about women's rights. We talked about her security needs and how obedience to God (who requires submission) was the route to personal fulfillment. Health, to the secular counselor, involved self-assertion. Health, to the biblical counselor, necessarily included self-denial and submission motivated not by weakness or fear, but by a loving trust in Christ.

Because the goal of counseling is distinctly dependent upon one's value system, and because there is a sizeable segment of our society committed to an evangelical Christian ethic, it seems clear that a system of biblical counseling has a necessary place in the world of professional counseling approaches. The Christian has one goal for his life — to become more like Christ. Paul preached in order to present every man mature in Christ. God has pledged Himself to reproduce His Son in each of us and we now are privileged to cooperate with Him in achieving that objective.

A biblical counselor will never excuse ungodly behavior or attitudes. Resentment, self-pity, immorality, envy, lack of contentment, materialistic strivings, lust, pride, lying, anxiety are all contrary to the image of Christ. The goal of the biblical counselor is to assist a person to change in the direction of Christlikeness. The basic interference with the maturing process is unbelief or, more precisely, wrong beliefs. Evidence that there is a problem is seen in negative, destructive emotions and behaviors. Another volume needs to be written on the actual techniques of changing beliefs and promoting "healthy" behaviors and feelings. It is not enough to say that the Holy Spirit will guide. If the counselor substitutes alleged Spirit-led counseling for hard thinking and careful procedure, the result invariably will be sloppy counseling. The purpose of this book is to lay the theoretical foundation for a biblically consistent approach to counseling, to provide a basis for hard thinking and careful procedure. It is my prayerful hope that

118

it will serve as a helpful stimulus in equipping Christian therapists and counselors to participate in the exciting task of presenting every man complete in Christ and that it will perhaps make a little clearer the role of the local church in meeting the deepest needs of the person.

Effective Biblical Counselling

How caring Christians can become capable counsellors

Dr Larry Crabb

In contrast to the inner-sanctum approach of private counselling, Dr Crabb offers a practical model of counselling for Christians within their local church, in which relationships based on caring, trust and acceptance are seen as an essential part of God's provision for our deepest human needs. This book will enable mature and caring Christians to become capable counsellors and will transform the quality of care offered by local churches everywhere.

'A landmark book to which I return again and again.'
SELWYN HUGHES

'Larry Crabb has written a clear and concise book which contains important insights, making it essential reading for all Christian counsellors. It should also be an invaluable resource for any church wanting to provide an effective lay counselling ministry for its congregation.'
MARY PYTCHES

'Larry Crabb's book has stood the test of time. It was one of the first to lay the foundations of a biblical basis for counselling and does so with the perceptive view that human beings need security and significance for true fulfilment. That sense of meaning, worth and love are found, Crabb argues, through a life transformed by Jesus Christ.'
ROGER HURDING

Understanding People

Reaching deeper through biblical counselling

Dr Larry Crabb

'How do we evaluate the dozens of approaches designed to help people solve their problems and live more effectively? Both the secular and the Christian communities are overrun with ideas about growth and wholeness. We want to know not only what will work, but…what is true and right.'

DR LARRY CRABB

So many contemporary models of counselling focus on individual freedom and fulfilment. This, argues Larry Crabb, does not satisfy a person's deepest longings for relationship – with others and, above all, with God.

Drawing on the insights gained from psychological inquiry, *Understanding People* offers a challenging, probing and realistic model of biblical counselling that has the power to transform Christian counselling and counsellors alike, and to help people towards life-changing intimacy and community.

Men and Women

Understanding how relationships work

Dr Larry Crabb

Few people today would challenge the equal worth of men and women at work, in the family or in their capacity for contributing to society. Yet has political correctness blurred essential differences that were designed to enrich the way that men and women relate to one another?

Larry Crabb probes the causes of what is perhaps the most overwhelming personal problem of our times – the breakdown of relationships between husbands and wives – and discovers a healthier, more positive and more authentically biblical pattern for giving and receiving love.

'A wise and liberating book.'
J. I. PACKER

Faith In A Changing Culture

Creating churches for the next century

John Drane

The last decade of this century has not been good news for the Church. The rapid rise of alternative spirituality is a direct challenge to orthodox Christianity. Increasingly, the Church is dismissed not only as being irrelevant and out-moded, but also as 'unspiritual'. In this ground-breaking book, John Drane explores how an authentic Christ-centred spirituality should be vital, attractive and relevant to twenty-first-century culture. He suggests that by reclaiming our biblical roots, where we are impacted afresh by the compelling presence of Christ in the gospels, and by understanding the forces which shape Western culture, we can create dynamic new patterns of worship, community and evangelism.

First published in 1994 as *Evangelism For A New Age*, and now revised, the message of John Drane's book has lost none of its edge as the millennium approaches.

John Drane is Director of the Centre for the Study of Christianity and Contemporary Society at the University of Stirling, and is an adjunct professor in the School of Theology at Fuller Seminary in California. His many books include *Happy Families?*, co-written with his wife Olive.

Being Human, Being Church

Spirituality and mission in the local church

Robert Warren

This seminal book will help define mission and evangelism in the next century.

To a greater or lesser extent, every church engages in three areas of experience: community, mission and worship. Where these three overlap, a church's spirituality can be found, argues Robert Warren. This is the pulsating heart beat that gives life and growth and enables individual Christians to engage with the culture that surrounds them courageously and creatively.

The problem for many churches is that there is a gaping hole where the very heart of their life should be. These are the churches that refuse to grow, that from the outside are perceived as having nothing to offer.

This exciting, innovative and practical book will help every church diagnose and treat those problems which stifle its spirituality and will empower members and leaders alike to become visionary, missionary congregations.

Canon Robert Warren is the Church of England's National Officer for the Decade of Evangelism. Formerly Rector of St Thomas Crookes in Sheffield, he is the author of three books.

The Shepherd Trilogy

Phillip Keller

Phillip Keller's three devotional classics – *A Shepherd Looks at the 23rd Psalm, A Shepherd Looks at the Good Shepherd* and *A Shepherd Looks at the Lamb of God* – are brought together in this omnibus edition.

As a shepherd, Phillip Keller knew what it was to protect a vulnerable flock on a daily basis. The special skills of a shepherd demanded compassion, care and guidance. As in all his writings, his own practical experience was a source of profound spiritual insight into the relationship between God and his people. These reflections on the most famous psalm of all, on the relationship between the Good Shepherd and his sheep, and the sacrificial role of Christ, the Lamb of God, are timeless.

Phillip Keller was born in East Africa. A deep love for the land drew him not only into a farming career but also into wildlife photography and journalism, and provided the inspiration for his devotional writings. A favourite Christian author for almost 30 years, he has written over 40 books.